The Mountain Bike Repair Handbook

THE
Mountain Bike Repair
HANDBOOK

Dennis Coello

Lyons & Burford,
PUBLISHERS

Printed in the United States of America

10 9 8 7 6 5 4 3 2

Library of Congress Cataloging-in-Publication Data

Coello, Dennis.
   The mountain bike repair handbook / Dennis Coello.
      p.   cm.
   ISBN 1-55821-064-4 : $12.95
   1. All terrain bicycles—Maintenance and repair. I. Title.
TL430.C63   1990
629.28'772—dc20   89-78484
                                                                         CIP

For Brad Hansen and Ken Gronseth

ACKNOWLEDGMENTS

This book is dedicated to the two mechanics who made it possible—Brad Hansen and Ken Gronseth. Their expertise is obvious in the following pages, and I thank them for all the time they spent answering my questions and proofing the manuscript. I should add that while they are responsible for the pages of detailed mechanical instructions, any problems that remain are my sole responsibility (and the result of my comparative lack of mechanical aptitude).

Thanks are also due to Dia Compe, Shimano, Specialized, and SunTour (for permission to reprint their excellent instruction sheets); to Kris Peterson, Mary Perkins, Dennis Nieweg, and Nate Bischoff for their drawings; and to Philip Blomquist, owner of Bicycle Center, for putting up with my constant presence around his shop.

CONTENTS

INTRODUCTION

Stroll through almost any bike shop or bookstore and you will soon discover that this is not the only bike mechanics book around. Larger stores will offer many: detailed shop manuals for professional mechanics, less-detailed texts for cyclists working on their bikes at home, books that claim to cover everything and some that purposefully focus just upon the problems one encounters on the road. Not only are there many mechanics books, but I wrote one several years ago (*Roadside Guide to Bike Repairs*) that was dedicated entirely to this subject and have also included lengthy chapters on mechanics in many of my other books.

With all the options already available a question no doubt comes to mind: Which book should you buy? Well, let me explain how this particular manual differs from the rest.

First, it is designed solely for the mountain biker. One can of course use this guide to repair those parts of thin-tire bikes that are very similar to ATBs (all-terrain bicycles), but the constant focus throughout has been the maintenance and repair of much-used fat-tire rigs. You know the ones I mean—the mud-encrusted trail bikes that are abused each weekend and hosed clean in car washes on Sunday night; the commuter bikes that see daily duty in the urban-jungle hell of potholes and sewer gratings, that stand at racks for hours in the rain and are lucky if their drive trains see oil once in a dozen storms. One of the greatest selling points of mountain bikes is their go-anywhere, anytime reliability. It's only natural, therefore, that owners should enjoy this fea-

1

ture to the point of excess. *The Mountain Bike Repair Handbook* attempts to counteract the damage.

The second great difference between this book and others is the way in which the information was compiled. Usually the author of such manuals is the kind of fellow who, in the late fifties and sixties (when I was growing up), was an out-of-it high school kid who not only understood what was going on in physics but spent his free time in a garage. And then, rather than progressing to the expected position of senior engineer at NASA, took the far more demanding route of keeping pace with (*and* fixing the problems that resulted from) those senior engineers who created bikes and bike components.

Those of you who know me through my other books realize that I, unfortunately, possess no such mechanical genius. Thus, you know that mechanics manuals are also written by another sort—equally out-of-it high schoolers who did *not* have a clue to what was going on in physics, and whose skill in bike mechanics came from a simple desperation born of the need to fix their bikes when they broke down far from home. Manuals written by the first group are usually extremely dry tomes of technowizardry, understood best by other engineer types who already know the essence of a cog. And while those written by the second group are normally easier to follow, they are, *ipso facto*, less comprehensive in approach.

Well, this book has combined the two types, That is, without any further understanding of mechanics beyond that gained through two additional decades of breakdowns, I have written a readable, comprehensive text and added mechanical insights known only to the NASA types. No, I've not discovered that I was actually Orville Wright in a former life. Nor have I simply plagiarized the shop manuals; I admit cracking a few, but found them unfathomable. My approach, instead, was first to ingratiate myself with two excellent bike-shop mechanics who for years have laughed at my attempts at repair. Next, after only a few weeks of the 'umble servant routine, I gained access to their inner sanctum—the bike-shop mechanics' bay. And third, after only a dozen or so requests, they agreed to let me record their answers to my questions, and their comments about the bikes brought through their door.

What a world opened to me. Each day I would appear with my cameras, microcassette recorder, and clipboard, begin pelting them with what I thought were intelligent queries, and endure the sneers of these gear wizards in their den. At least once each hour they would erupt with derisive laughter or contempt when a much-abused mountain bike was wheeled inside, or when I diagnosed a problem incorrectly. But their harshest remarks were saved for the manufacturer representatives whose products made their lives more difficult—those that through poor design or failure to anticipate possible mistreatment by riders, couldn't take the pounding inherent in the life of an ATB.

The result is what you have before you, a simple maintenance and repair guide written for the nonexpert (even first-time) all-terrain bike mechanic, but with the additional insights of those who really, really understand how a derailleur works *and* who see the results of hard riding (and even harder landings) on a daily basis. Their location in Utah makes them the recipients of bikes fresh from the batterings of tough Rocky Mountain alpine trails, as well as those still coated with the red earth and fine, corrosive sand of deserts to the south. And, of course, they have the experience of repairing their own and many other bikes that reach them fresh from southern Utah's famed (and infamous) Slickrock Trail.

Oh yes—the third major difference between this and other mechanic guides. With the firm belief that visual aids in such books are most often of more value than text, I have kept words to a minimum and substituted page after page of photographs, drawings, and "expanded-view" diagrams (graciously contributed by SunTour, Shimano, Specialized, and Dia Compe).

And so a final word before we begin. Shake from your mind any thoughts that you can't master what follows, that replacing a broken spoke and re-truing a wheel, for example, require the skills of a mechanical guru. Just proceed slowly, attempt to think clearly, and if you fail the first time around, expend your frustrations on something (preferably inanimate) *other* than your tools or bike. All the best.

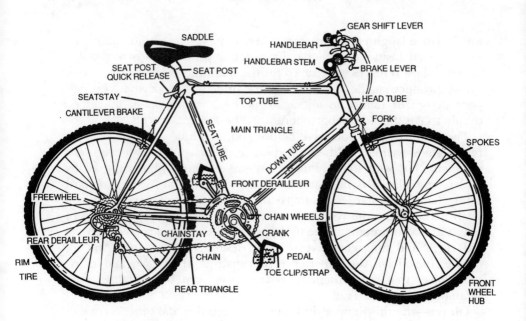

SADDLE

GEAR SHIFT LEVER

HANDLEBAR

HANDLEBAR STEM

BRAKE LEVER

SEAT POST
QUICK RELEASE

SEAT POST

SEATSTAY

HEAD TUBE

TOP TUBE

CANTILEVER BRAKE

FORK

SEAT TUBE

MAIN TRIANGLE

SPOKES

DOWN TUBE

FRONT DERAILLEUR

FREEWHEEL

CHAIN WHEELS

REAR DERAILLEUR

CHAINSTAY

CRANK

RIM

CHAIN

PEDAL

TIRE

TOE CLIP/STRAP

REAR TRIANGLE

FRONT
WHEEL
HUB

1

TOOLS

I t's a common question: What tools should I take on the trail and during commutes? I know what I pack along, but because I've been chastised so often for hauling too much gear I'll let the experts have their say first. Our mechanics—Brad Hansen and Ken Gronseth—who by the way are themselves excellent mountain bikers, suggest the following as an absolute minimum:

TIRE LEVERS

SPARE TUBE AND PATCH KIT

AIR PUMP

ALLEN WRENCHES: 3, 4, 5, and 6 mm

SIX-INCH CRESCENT: adjustable-end wrench

SMALL SCREWDRIVER: flat-blade tip

CHAIN RIVET TOOL

SPOKE WRENCH

However, their *personal* tool pouches contain (in addition to the above):

CHANNEL LOCKS: with handles sawn off to approximately 6 inches

AIR GAUGE: pencil-type; when pushing tires to lowest possible pressures it is important to be accurate

TUBE VALVE CAP: metal kind, with valve-stem remover

Mechanics Ken Gronseth (left) and Brad Hansen.

BALING WIRE: a ten-inch length; good for temporary repair if something big breaks

DUCT TAPE: small five-foot roll; good for temporary repair if something small breaks, can also be used as tire boot if nothing better is present

BOOT MATERIAL: a small piece of old sew-up tire works best; large tube patch is a good substitute

SPARE CHAIN LINK

REAR DERAILLEUR PULLEY

SPARE NUTS AND BOLTS

PAPER TOWEL AND TUBE OF WATERLESS HAND CLEANER

For my longer, heavily laden rides I add to the list extra spokes, freewheel tool, cone wrenches, cotterless-crank removal tools, and a pocket vise (or chain whip or "Cassette Cracker," whichever tool is required to replace broken spokes on the freewheel side), but then I'm the only person I know who has had trouble with spokes breaking on a mountain bike. I attribute that solely to one poorly laced wheel I had on tour (for I've never broken one since), and to the fact that I almost never ride without an accompanying waist pack and panniers filled with at least twenty-five pounds of photographic gear. In short, hit the trails with the tools listed above and you'll be in fine shape, *as long as you start out with a bike in good working order.*

A second question inevitably follows the first of which tools should be taken on trail, long tour, and commuting rides: Which are necessary for *home* repair and maintenance? The answer of course entails a considerably longer list, especially if you plan, in time, to end costly bikeshop visits.

1. CRESCENT WRENCH—15 INCHES: If you do not have a large vise at home or work or have easy access to one, a large crescent (or pipe wrench in a pinch) will serve to remove a locked-tight freewheel.

2. CRESCENT WRENCH—6 INCHES: Shop mechanics view crescents with disdain because of the rounding of nuts and bolt heads that is possible when torque is applied. But not all of us can afford a full set of metric open- or box-end wrenches. Besides, you'll need a six-inch (a *good* six-inch, where the slide mechanism turns freely and precisely to hold the jaws against a nut) for the road.

3. CRESCENT WRENCH—4 INCHES: Ken and Brad eye my preference for such a tool with only slightly veiled scorn, but then I do not possess the proper metric wrenches nor the manual dexterity or expertise they employ when dealing with the smaller fittings on brakes and derailleurs. Mountain-bike-component manufacturers have taken giant steps in substituting allen-head fittings in place of nuts and bolts, but with the smaller nut-and-bolt fittings that remain I prefer the more precise feel granted by a four-inch crescent to the six-inch I employ for larger work.

4. CHANNEL LOCKS—7 INCHES: This is an excellent tool for tightening headsets and for gripping anything too large for the six-inch crescent.

5. VISE GRIPS: There's no better way to remove rounded-off bolts.

6. REGULAR-BLADE SCREWDRIVER: Choose one that has a high-quality thin-steel tip. It should be short-handled and long-shanked so your hand won't obscure your view during precise derailleur adjustments and when using the thin tip to pry up rubber and plastic bearing seals.

7. NEEDLE-NOSE PLIERS: I use a small pair with side-cutters for trimming brake and gear cables. The mechanics use a longer-nosed pair when doing bearing work on pedals.

8. ALLEN (HEX) WRENCHES: Hit the trails without the proper wrench for every allen head on your bike and the Fates will surely cause that single bolt you've overlooked to loosen up. Also, do not try to get by with an allen that "almost" fits; you'll end up rounding off the corners and ruining the bolt.

9. CONE WRENCHES: Shops use high-quality, very sturdy cone wrenches that weigh much more than the two spindly, lightweight wrenches I pack along on tour. If you plan only day rides and commutes you probably won't be packing these wrenches and therefore might prefer to purchase the shop models, which last forever.

10. TIRE LEVERS: The mechanics and I were in complete agreement on needing only two of the three levers sold, unfortunately, as a set. (What a great way to make us buy an unnecessary item!) However, while I (for sentimental reasons) still pack the heavy-steel models I carried on my world ride in 1974, the gurus have gone to molded plastic.

11. SWISS ARMY KNIFE: I carry one on tour because its multiple blades and attachments serve a thousand and one unexpected purposes. Any sharp blade, or an extremely thin screwdriver tip, will suffice to pry up bearing seals.

12. CHAIN RIVET TOOL: This is necessary to remove a chain or add or subtract links. I once thought it was required to free frozen links as well, until the mechanics showed me the simple technique of hand manipulation.

13. SPOKE NIPPLE WRENCH: The "T" type is pictured; this model, and the "hoop" style wrench, are my preferences over the round multi-size-nipple wrenches. Make sure the wrench you purchase will fit your spokes.

14. FREEWHEEL TOOL: Don't go out and buy one until you are sure your freewheel model requires it. Unfortunately (at least for those who must work on many bikes), cassette hubs and the newest drive-chain systems have greatly increased the number of freewheel-removal techniques.

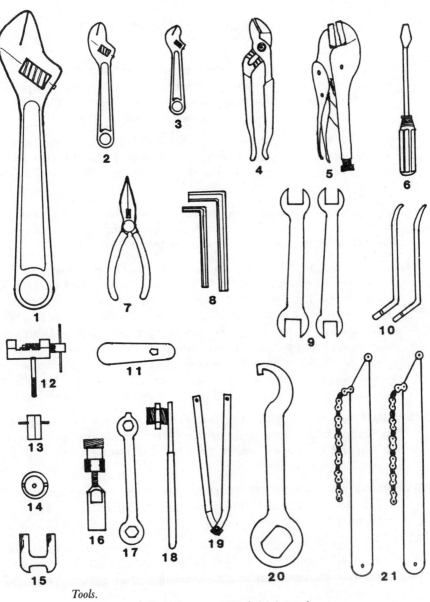

Tools.

1) crescent wrench—15"
2) crescent wrench—6"
3) crescent wrench—4"
4) channel locks—7"
5) vise grips
6) regular blade screwdriver
7) needle-nose pliers
8) allen wrenches
9) cone wrenches
10) tire levers
11) Swiss Army Knife

12) chain rivet tool
13) spoke nipple wrench
14) freewheel tool
15) pocket vise
16) cotterless crank removal tool
17) universal cotterless crank wrench
18) universal cotterless crankarm puller
19) universal adjustable cup tool
20) lock ring/fixed cup bottom bracket tool
21) freewheel sprocket tools

15. POCKET VISE: Again, do not buy one until you learn whether it can be used with your particular freewheel. If your system accepts it you'll find this vise invaluable because it will take the place of a large home vise or fifteen-inch crescent while on the road.

16. COTTERLESS-CRANK REMOVAL TOOLS: Most riders pack these crank-specific tools on all-terrain tours and—if theirs is the only bike they ever service—use them at home in place of the following universals.

17. UNIVERSAL COTTERLESS-CRANK WRENCH: Necessary for the bottom bracket bearing service on cranks of various sizes. This tool, and the following universal, are too heavy to carry on a bike.

18. UNIVERSAL COTTERLESS-CRANKARM PULLER: The previous tool removes the "crankarm fixing bolt" (that wonderful advance of technology beyond the formerly ubiquitous—and hated—cotter pins); this tool pulls the crankarm to allow access to the bottom bracket hub. Again, unless you plan to work on several cranks, you can get by with the multipurpose nonuniversal removal tool (#16 above). (*Note:* the Sugino "Autex" crankarm bolt-puller system employs a special dust cap that requires only a 6 mm allen wrench. These are great for the road and might be all you require at home as well.)

19. UNIVERSAL ADJUSTABLE CUP TOOL: This is excellent for home use, but far too heavy for the road. Only on my longest tours do I work on my bottom bracket, and then I use a screwdriver blade tip to adjust the bottom bracket bearing pressure.

20. LOCK RING/FIXED CUP BOTTOM BRACKET TOOL: For adjustments of the bottom bracket lock ring and fixed cup. It is far too large to carry on a bike.

21. FREEWHEEL SPROCKET TOOLS: These are necessary to remove the freewheels of some new systems and are of use with all freewheels when one wishes to replace a worn-out cog or make changes to alter gearing.

22. SEALED-BEARING TOOLS/ROLLER CAM BRAKE TOOL (not pictured): Most mountain bikes have "sealed" (actually "shielded" in most cases) bearings in one or more areas—pedals, headset, hubs, bottom bracket. The tools required for their maintenance are discussed as these components are encountered in later chapters.

If you find yourself spending a good number of hours working on your bike you'll soon begin longing for that item that makes such work so much easier—a tune-up stand. Wheel-truing stands are more in the realm of the aficionado; thin-tire cyclists usually purchase these long before mountain bikers feel the need. In the quarter century since I took my first tour I have never owned one, finding it possible to true my wheels well enough using the chainstay/thumb-guide method described in the next chapter. However, it doesn't matter which kind of tires you ride when it comes to the need for a floor pump with built-in gauge and flip-off nozzle. Hand pumps are a time-consuming pain.

2
WHEELS

In the fall and winter of 1988 I spent nearly three months pedaling some twenty-five hundred miles through the Rockies, from the Canadian border to Santa Fe. I was on thin tires for the first half, but by the time I reached southern Wyoming the snows had grown too deep; I ducked into Salt Lake, grabbed a mountain bike, and rode the last fifteen hundred or so on interlocking center-rib knobbies.

The point of this is not to tell you how I spent my winter vacation. It is, instead, to say that on that ride, and for the past few years of almost daily riding (commutes, trails, tours, and many fully loaded photo shoots), I have not had a flat on my mountain bike.

I attribute my good fortune to several factors: commuting with tire liners (thin, nearly impenetrable plastic sheaths that sit between the tire and tube, protecting the latter from puncture); riding with good rubber (*not* riding with nearly\bald, worn-out tires); and frequent checks for proper tire inflation. But I *have* had flats and will, no doubt, in the future, and, according to our mechanics, they remain the single greatest problem for bikers at large.

Because of this fact we will begin our repairs with punctures. And I might add that although I can for the most part repeat the directions I provided in my book *The Complete Mountain Biker*, I will also give slight variations and diagnostic techniques supplied by Ken and Brad as I watched them fix a flat.

Cantilever brake being released for wheel removal.

FLATS

Tools required:

2 TIRE LEVERS (also called "spoons")

6-INCH CRESCENT WRENCH (if your wheels aren't quick-release)

TUBE REPAIR KIT or spare tube

AIR PUMP

Chances are your flat will be in the rear because of the greater weight this wheel carries and because it is the drive wheel on the bike. We will therefore discuss rear-tire repair; all directions apply to the front tire also except, of course, for those involving derailleur, chain movement, and freewheel removal. (I *know* that most of you already knew that, and because you're already mad at having a flat it scarcely helps to read unnecessary sentences. Please remember that this is a book for the greenest beginner as well as you.)

First, shift the chain onto the smallest freewheel sprocket to assist in wheel removal. Next, disengage the rear brake so as to spread the brake pads from the rim sufficiently to let the tire pass between them. (When engaged, the pads of properly adjusted brakes sit very close to the rim—too close to allow for wheel removal.)

How is this accomplished? If you have cantilever or U-brakes you should be able to reach under the rim (between the spokes), squeeze the pads toward each other, grab hold of the small knob at the end of the brake cable, and lift it free. If your brakes are powercam, squeeze the pads together as before and twist the cam (the X-shaped metal plate between both brake arms) free.

So you've tried this and can't manage it? Later, after reading the chapter on brake repair, you will be able to set up your brakes so this is possible (by slackening your cable slightly). For now, however, you can employ a small crescent or box/open-end wrench or allen to remove one brake shoe and thereby remove the wheel—once you have flipped the quick-release lever or loosened the axle nuts and, taking hold of the derailleur body, pulled it back toward you (thus moving the upper-jockey-pulley away from the freewheel cogs). Wheels often become

Derailleur body being pulled back for wheel removal.

Single tire lever hooked onto spoke.

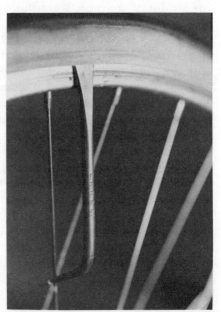

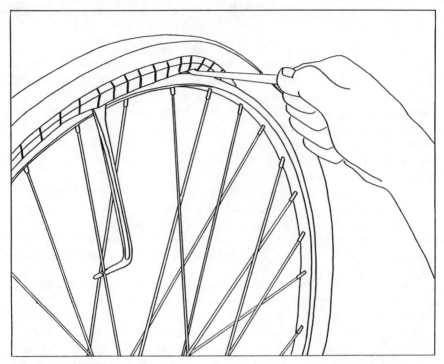

Tire levers at work.

stuck in their dropouts (that portion of the frame that holds the wheel axles) and may require a sharp rap with the heel of the hand near the top of the tire to dislodge them.

When you have lifted the wheel free from the frame, let all remaining air out of the tube. You will probably have Schrader valves on your bike (the automobile-type valves); the air is released by depressing the tiny metal shaft in the center of the round valve. Now take the non-hook end (usually the lesser-angled end) of one tire lever and, beveled side up, work it underneath the bead. (Begin working with this first lever at a point on the wheel *opposite* the valve stem.) Push down (toward the spokes) on the tire lever in your hand. Hook the slotted lever side onto a spoke to hold it and the tire in place (notice drawing). This frees both hands for the next step.

With the second lever, work the tip beneath the tire bead about an inch or so from the first lever. Again, push down to pop the bead away from its seat in the rim. If you can't do this, move the tire lever slightly closer to the first. Now continue to work the bead away from the rim all around the wheel, until one side of the tire is completely free.

At this point I begin working one of the spoons from the opposite side of the wheel, manipulating the second bead off the rim. (You are now working the bead off the rim *away* from you in direction because both beads must come off the same side to free the tire.) Taking one side of the tire off at a time is much easier than trying to force both beads off at once. Expect a new tire to be more difficult to remove than an old one. However, ATB tires are much easier to peel off than racing or thin-tire touring rubber, old or new.

The mechanics have a slightly different procedure, which I had never seen before. Rather than removing the second tire bead, the tire is allowed to remain on the rim and the tube is simply pulled free. The purpose of this technique is not, as I supposed, for the time saved in omitting complete tire removal. It is instead to allow for tube/tire orientation that, in the case of extremely slow leaks, tells the rider where to search his tube once the culprit tack or thorn has been found in the casing.

My personal method of finding such protrusions is to overlap my fingers inside the casing and spin them around the circumference of the tire, but a particular drawback should be noted. I have, on occasion, run a finger into a thorn or shard of glass a bit too quickly. You might wish to consider a somewhat slower technique.

The mechanics also stated that the *kind* of hole in the tube should be seen as a diagnostic tool (albeit a rather crude one) hinting at what caused the flat. A single hole is usually something coming through the tire casing; a "snakebite" hole is the result of "rim pinch"—where underinflation or tremendous force has caused the wheel rim to pinch the tube against an object. In the latter case one will not, of course, find anything puncturing the tire wall.

With the tube out of the tire, inflate it until firm and somewhat fat, but (in Ken's words) "Not so that it looks like a bloated snake. You run a chance of blowing it up." Now listen for escaping air. Only twice in my life have I had to hold a tube under water to find a pinprick hole by following escaping air bubbles to the source. And only *once* in a quarter century of serious pedaling have I found the extremely slow leak to be the result of a valve core. (If your tube has a Schrader valve, be sure the air is not escaping from the threaded center valve core. If this core is not screwed tightly into these threads an air leak will result. The proper tool to tighten a valve core is the valve cover tool, a tiny slotted metal cap you should buy to replace the worthless black plastic caps present

Ken listening for air escaping from tube.

on all the tubes sold.)

Once, when I located a hole, if it was small I would circle it closely with a ballpoint pen. While I cannot recall this ever causing problems, Brad and Ken explained what I should have thought of long ago: Ink can cause a patch to fail to adhere around the edges if one fails to rough up the tube beyond the inked circle. To mark a tiny hole they use ballpoints, but instead of a circle they draw three arrows pointing toward the site, ending them more than a patch-length distant.

When the hole is located and marked, let all the air out (you don't want any blowing out the hole while you're applying the patch) and rough up the area—in one direction only—with the patch-kit scraper. Be sure to do a good job of it, short of putting additional holes in the tube, and be sure to roughen an area a bit larger than the size of the patch.

Apply the glue (I use a somewhat-clean finger), a bit more than necessary to cover the patch area. Most kits suggest waiting until the glue is dry to apply the patch. So, wait. Hurry this step and there's a good chance you'll be taking the wheel off the bike again a few miles down the road. Be careful not to touch the patch side that goes on the tube and, beginning at patch center and running toward the edges, press the patch with a spoon or the rounded end of another tool. In this manner you will drive out any remaining air bubbles.

When the patch appears to be holding well along the edges, pump a very slight amount of air into the tube to avoid wrinkles when it's placed back inside the tire. Put the tube in the tire (Ken and Brad suggest "dusting" the top of the patch with dirt—unless you happen to have talc with you—so as to keep the patch from adhering to the tire casing in future), then push the valve stem through the valve-stem hole in the rim and reseat one of the beads (using a tire lever with the beveled side down). Once one side of the tire—one bead—is back in place, begin reseating the second bead. (Removing all air at this point reduces the chance of puncture.) In taking off a tire one begins *opposite* the stem; in replacing it one begins work at the stem and works away from it in both directions, being sure to keep the stem pointing straight up. Riders who fail to do this, or who ride with low air pressure in their tires (which causes the tube to shift and the valve stem to angle out of the hole), cause wearing of the stem along its side and base. Once a hole occurs in the valve stem the entire tube is shot, for stems can't hold a patch.

Applying glue to tube. Patches shown at right.

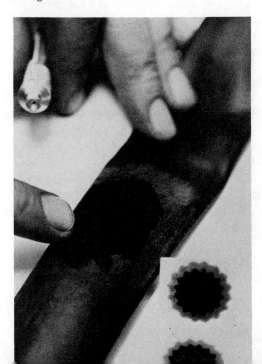

With new thin tires I can usually restore by hand all of the second bead except for about six inches, and then must resort to a spoon. ATB tires, especially after their first time off and on the rim, can sometimes be installed and removed without any tools at all.

I must admit to being surprised while watching Ken and Brad pump in perhaps ten pounds psi, then spend a solid minute inspecting both sides of the rim for "tube pinch"—the presence of the tube between the rim and tire bead. They did this by peeling back the bead slightly and looking for the tube peeking underneath. I explained that I had never had this problem, but both said they had, that it is of course fatal once full air pressure is restored, and that one must be especially cautious of this if blowing up a tire with a carbon-dioxide cartridge. If you do have a pinched tube, let all the air out and work the tube back (carefully!) under the bead with a spoon. Preferable to this, if you can manage it, is making the tube slip back up inside the tire casing by rocking the tire backward at the point of tube pinch, thereby lifting the tire bead slightly. Or, take off the tire completely and start afresh.

If both beads are properly seated and the stem is still perpendicular, inflate the tire to desired pressure (doing so before restoring it to the bike frame saves one step in case you've goofed with the patch; inexpensive tires on cheap rims, I was told, can sometimes unseat themselves during reinflation) and restore the wheel to the frame. Do so by once again pulling the derailleur cage back toward you and out of the way, then dropping the smallest freewheel cog into the chain and settling the axle into the dropouts. Look down the back of the tire toward the bottom bracket (the point where chainstays and seat tube meet) to center the wheel. More expensive bikes will center it automatically when you pull the axle back to the dropout "stops." Close the quick-release (q-r) lever or tighten the axle nuts, *restore your rear brake to working order,* and take off.

But first a word on the quick release. It is *not* a nut with a handle. If properly set you should begin encountering stiffness on the lever when closing it to half-mast position or slightly further. It should not be so difficult to close that it requires pounding, and having to grip the seatstay with the fingers while depressing the q-r lever with the heel of that hand will leave the lever parallel to the seatstay tube—an extremely difficult position for opening the lever the next time you need to remove your wheel. If you find that pounding or gripping the frame tube is necessary to close the lever, back it off (make it easier to close) by loosening the bale nut on the other side of the frame.

BROKEN SPOKES

Tools required:

SPOKE WRENCH

6-INCH CRESCENT (to remove rear-wheel axle nuts, if your wheel is not quick-release)

TIRE LEVERS (not required if old spoke nipple can be used, and if wheel truing is done with tire in place)

FREEWHEEL-REMOVAL TOOL (if break is on the freewheel side requiring freewheel removal; see below for special tools required with particular freewheel systems)

PATIENCE (a great deal, especially if this is your first time around)

You will notice from the list above that you are expected to break spokes only on the rear wheel, and then only on the freewheel side. Actually, you will probably *never* break a spoke, this being an affliction primarily of overloaded thin-tire tourers and of thin-tire commuters who fall into the hungry jaws of sewer gratings.

The most common reasons for spokes breaking on ATBs are: 1. a poorly adjusted derailleur that shifts the chain from the largest freewheel cog into the spokes, thereby chewing up spoke heads (if your "pie plate"—spoke protector—fails to do its job); and 2. a rock or log striking the rear derailleur and shoving it into the spokes. Ouch.

Ninety percent of the spokes that break for no apparent reason break on the freewheel side. Why? Because of the far greater stress (greater tension) under which those spokes wheel through life compared to the far luckier spokes on the flip side of the rim. You'll understand if you take a look at your wheel. Notice how the spokes on the freewheel side run from the rim to the wheel flange (where they attach) at a much greater angle than those on the other wheel side? This is necessitated by the presence of the freewheel and the length of axle it takes up.

Glance at your front wheel for a moment. Notice how the spokes radiate in perfect proportion. *This,* not just the added weight on the rear wheel compared to the front, is the reason front wheel spokes almost never snap. The word describing the steeper angle of freewheel-side spokes is "dishing"; a lesser-dished wheel is preferable to one with greater dishing, at least as far as spoke life is concerned.

Unfortunately, at least for spokes, the transformation of freewheels from five to six, and now *seven* sprockets, has brought on spacing (*ergo* dishing) problems that have been handled, in part, by thinner chains. (A thinner chain requires less space between cogs and thus takes up less space overall on the axle.) Again, the beefier tires and rims on good-quality mountain bikes will probably keep you from breaking spokes no matter how many cogs are on your freewheel. It is instead a problem more for those who might wish to switch from a five- to seven-speed (cog) freewheel. Ken mentioned that he had done that only a few months before, establishing the not uncommon setup of one hundred kilograms of spoke tension on his freewheel side, between sixty and seventy on the other. On the first tough trail ride he potato-chipped his wheel, was able to ride home due to his ever-present and well-supplied tool kit, and backed off to a six-cog freewheel for more equal dishing. Now all is well.

Freewheel and Cog Removal

Okay, by this point you understand spokes a bit more, and perhaps appreciate their lot in life. But you've still got one broken, probably on the freewheel side of your rear wheel, and must get around to fixing it. Unless you have extremely high-flange hubs, there is no chance of wiggling a replacement spoke between the cogs and into the spoke hole, so you will have to remove your freewheel.

Begin by removing the wheel, as described earlier. Next, ascertain what kind of freewheel you have and obtain the necessary tools. These will be: *On old-style freewheels*—a freewheel-removal tool and vise (or large crescent or pipe wrench, or pocket vise if on the road). *On non-hyperglide cassette freewheels*—two freewheel sprocket tools (also called "chain whips") or, on the road, a "Cassette Cracker" (*Note:* Neither the mechanics nor I have yet used this new tool, described as "A mini-whip tool for on-the-road disassembly of rear hub cassettes.") *On hyperglide cassette freewheels*—a freewheel-removal tool and vise (or medium-size crescent or pipe wrench, or pocket vise if on the road), or freewheel-removal tool and one chain whip.

Confused? Well, don't be; just concentrate on your particular system and forget the rest.

First, with all models, remove the quick-release skewer or freewheel-side axle nuts. With the **old-style freewheel,** and if you have a vise around, place the correct freewheel-removal tool (teeth up) in the vise

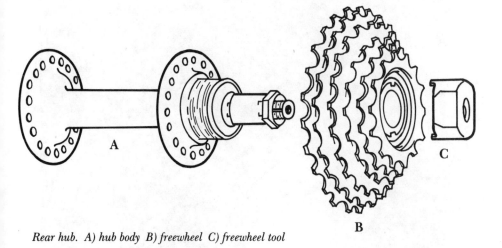

Rear hub. A) hub body B) freewheel C) freewheel tool

and settle the rear wheel onto it. Make sure the freewheel-tool's teeth match up with the freewheel and are fully engaged. When this is known, take hold of the wheel, press downward, and twist (counterclockwise) making sure not to rock the wheel so as to cause the tool and freewheel to slip apart.

The very low gears on mountain bikes make it possible to apply tremendous torque to the very sprocket you are attempting to break free (in the opposite direction, of course, than that in which you've been tightening it every time you've pedaled in that gear). Be prepared, therefore, and especially if you are a strong rider, to turn the wheel mightily before you succeed in breaking it free. When you have done so the freewheel will spin easily, by hand, off the hub.

And if there is no vise around? The next best method employs a fifteen-inch crescent or large pipe wrench. Fit the freewheel tool into the freewheel, attach the wrench, and—while standing over the wheel with it in front of you and the wrench to the right—push *down*. (Ken's analogy is apt; he says when people get confused about the direction in which a freewheel screws off he tells them to think of the wheel as a large jar of peanut butter, with the freewheel as its cap.)

Note that in the photograph the wrench is placed so that the greatest amount of pressure is applied against the full steel head of the wrench, not against the far weaker slide mechanism. You may also note that the quick-release bale nut is present, though I mentioned some paragraphs

Large crescent wrench on freewheel tool.

ago to remove the quick-release skewer (in case you have never done so, this is accomplished very easily by unscrewing both the bale nut and handle while holding the skewer—the rod—still). This is because *my* method has always been to remove that mechanism, taking care to hold the wrench and tool in line with the freewheel face when exerting force. The mechanics, however, use the q-r skewer to keep the free-

Freewheel tool in pocket vise.

wheel tool from slipping by cinching (not tightly) the bale nut against it. This is a good idea, it seems to me, provided you do not forget to remove the bale nut *immediately* upon breaking (loosening) the freewheel the first little bit. Forget this and you will strip the q-r skewer threads, or more likely break the skewer shaft.

From the drawing of the pocket vise you should be able to visualize the freewheel tool sitting snugly in the top, the wheel (and freewheel) balanced upon it, and the two bottom extensions of the pocket vise straddling a handlebar or highway guardrail. You then turn the wheel as you did when using a regular shop vise (counterclockwise), while attempting to keep anything from slipping free. The directions that

Two chain whip tools around freewheel.

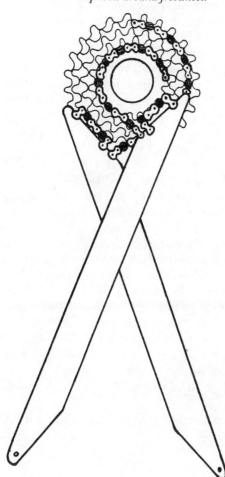

come with the pocket vise suggest running the quick-release skewer through the vise and freewheel tool and freewheel, then connecting it all with the bale nut to hold it in place. But note that if you are riding with solid axles (no q-r wheels), you will need to drill out the tiny (q-r-lever sized) hole running through the pocket vise to make it accept the larger axle.

Now let's turn to **nonhyperglide cassette freewheel systems.** Gaining access to the spoke holes in your wheel flange (hidden behind the freewheel cogs) with this system again requires removal of the cassette freewheel. This is most easily accomplished if you have two chain whips (sprocket tools). Wrap one chain whip around the smallest sprocket so that you can apply pressure in a counterclockwise direction; wrap the second in a clockwise direction around the second-largest cog. Notice that the tools have a device (on the same rod end as the chain, but on the oppopsite side) to engage the sprocket and hold fast between the teeth, *or* a second and much smaller whip of chain to hold the cog teeth (see drawing). Hold these tools as much in line (parallel to one another and the cogs) as possible, and push them toward each other.

The smallest cog, and usually the second smallest, will be unscrewed from the freewheel body; all remaining cogs on most freewheels can be lifted free as a unit or individually (by loosening the holding nuts on the bottom end of three long, thin bolts that reach through the cogs on some bodies to hold them in place).

This will all be a bit confusing at first and will take a few moments before each length of chain is wrapped correctly to allow for cog movement in the correct direction. Again, just remember the peanut-butter-jar analogy. You are looking at the lid.

A time-consuming and somewhat desperate second method of removing this kind of freewheel, resorted to only if chain whips, or home, are very far away, is to remove the entire axle from the wheel side opposite the freewheel, then insert a ten-millimeter allen wrench into the freewheel-body-fixing bolt (located smack in the freewheel center), and unscrew (counterclockwise).

Far preferable to this, and to the weight and space considerations involved in packing two sprocket tools on the bike, is the "Cassette Cracker—rear hub cassette tool." This "mini-whip" is said to provide relatively easy on-the-road disassembly of cassette hubs, and is offered by Pamir Engineering, Box 942B, Boyleston, Massachusetts 01505 (508) 869-2795.

Finally, we come to the removal of **hyperglide cassette freewheels.**

HIGH PRECISION LABYRINTH SEAL

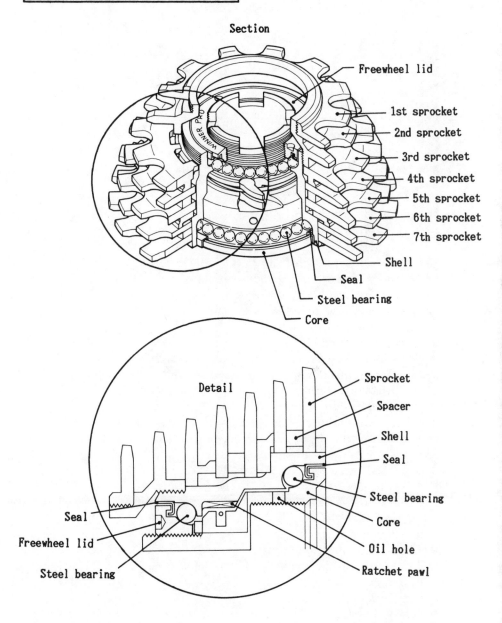

Section

Freewheel lid

1st sprocket
2nd sprocket
3rd sprocket
4th sprocket
5th sprocket
6th sprocket
7th sprocket

Shell

Seal

Steel bearing

Core

Detail

Sprocket

Spacer

Shell

Seal

Steel bearing

Core

Oil hole

Ratchet pawl

Seal

Freewheel lid

Steel bearing

Courtesy of SunTour USA, Inc.

SERVICE INSTRUCTION

Freehubs

SHIMANO DEORE XT FH-M732

SHIMANO DEORE LX FH-MT62

mountain LX FH-M452

Before use, read these instructions carefully, and follow them for correct use.

■ Specifications

	FH-M732	FH-MT62	FH-M452
Weight+	810g	760g	755g
Material	Light alloy and steel		
Suitable chain size	CN-M732/CN-MT62		
Spoke hole diameter	2.6mm		
Number of spoke holes	36H/32H		
Number of HG sprocket teeth	B-group: 12-14-16-18-21-24-28T		
	C-group: 13-15-17-20-23-26-30T		
Over lock nut dimension	130mm (5-1/8")/135mm (5-5/16")		

+ The HG sprocket's combination of teeth weight was measured at the B-group.

■ Notes

● In order to maintain smooth shifting performance of the HG (Hyper-Glide) sprocket, do not use a B-group and C-group sprocket combination. (Use each group as a 7-piece set.)

● For freehubs (FH-M732/FH-MT62/FH-M452) for the HG sprocket, former UG sprockets (CS-6400/CS-1000) can be used, but do not combine the HG sprocket and UG sprocket.

* Please note: Specifications are subject to change for improvement without notice.　　(English)

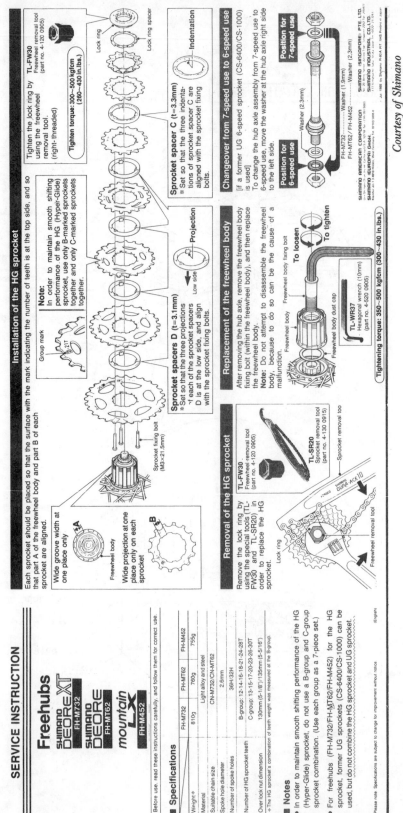

Installation of the HG sprocket

Each sprocket should be placed so that the surface with the mark indicating the number of teeth is at the top side, and so that part A of the freewheel body and part B of each sprocket are aligned.

Note:
In order to maintain smooth shifting performance of the HG (Hyper-Glide) sprocket, use only B-marked sprockets together and only C-marked sprockets together.

Group mark

Wide groove width at one place only

Freewheel body

Wide projection at one place only on each sprocket

Sprocket fixing bolt (M3×21.5mm)

Sprocket spacers D (t=3.1mm)
※ Set so that the three projections of each of the sprocket spacers D is at the low side, and align with the sprocket fixing bolts.

Projection — Low side

Sprocket spacer C (t=3.3mm)
※ Set so that the three indentations of sprocket spacer C are aligned with the sprocket fixing bolts.

Indentation

Lock ring

Lock ring spacer

Tighten the lock ring by using the freewheel removal tool. (right-threaded)

Tighten torque: 300~500 kgfcm (260~430 in.lbs.)

TL-FW30 Freewheel removal tool (part no. 4-120 0905)

Removal of the HG sprocket

Remove the lock ring by using the special tools (TL-FW30 and TL-SR20). In order to replace the HG sprocket.

Lock ring

TL-FW30 Freewheel removal tool (part no. 4-120 0905)

TL-SR20 Sprocket removal tool (part no. 4-130 0915)

Sprocket removal tool

Freewheel removal tool

Replacement of the freewheel body

After removing the hub axle, remove the freewheel body fixing bolt (within the freewheel body), and then replace the freewheel body.

Note: Do not attempt to disassemble the freewheel body, because to do so can be the cause of a malfunction.

Freewheel body fixing bolt

Freewheel body

Freewheel body dust cap

TL-WR37 Hexagonal wrench (10mm) (part no. 4-520 0905)

To loosen — To tighten

Tightening torque: 350~500 kgfcm (300~430 in.lbs.)

Changeover from 7-speed use to 6-speed use

[If a former UG 6-speed sprocket (CS-6400/CS-1000) is used]
To change the hub axle assembly from 7-speed use to 6-speed use, move the washer at the hub axle right side to the left side.

Position for 6-speed use

Position for 7-speed use

Washer (2.3mm)

Washer (2.3mm) — Washer (1.9mm)

FH-M732 .... Washer (2.3mm)
FH-MT62 / FH-M452 ...... Washer (2.3mm)

SHIMANO AMERICAN CORPORATION

SHIMANO (EUROPA) GmbH.

SHIMANO (SINGAPORE) PTE. LTD.

SHIMANO INDUSTRIAL CO.,LTD.

Jul. 1988 By Shimano. Printed in Japan

Courtesy of Shimano

The difference between these and other cassettes, at least as far as removal is concerned, lies in the presence of a freewheel lockring. This sits at the outer edge of the cogs, holding them in place (for none of the hyperglide sprockets screw onto the cassette body). Removal is therefore similar to the old-style noncassette freewheel, for the lockring is splined (grooved) to accept a Shimano Uniglide freewheel-removal tool. Insert the tool into the lockring and follow the directions given above for the removal of noncassette systems. Or use a single chain whip to hold the cogs in place while loosening (in a counterclockwise direction) the lockring.

Once removed, the individual cogs may be lifted free, thereby exposing the wheel flange for spoke replacement. The freewheel body is removed as with other cassettes, by inserting a ten-millimeter allen wrench into the cassette center (after the axle is withdrawn) and turning it counterclockwise. By the way, if you have any experience with old-style freewheels you will notice that the lockring is much easier to break free. This is because the ring is not tightened when one pedals because the chain does not engage the ring itself.

And a note to the wise owners of *any* freewheel system, and for that matter to would-be mechanics working away on all parts of a bike. As you remove anything, let's say in this case the sprockets and spacers between freewheels, lay the components out on a newspaper or shop cloth *in exact order*. Your shifting will be greatly affected if you rebuild the freewheel with cogs wrong-side-up.

Freewheel Core/Cassette Maintenance

When it comes to cleaning a freewheel, the body, or "core," can be disassembled, but I suggest this only if you make watches for a living. My extremely lazy alternative is to set the freewheel upside down (smallest sprocket to the ground) on many sheets of folded newspaper. Now flush the core with Liquid Wrench. This is done by shooting the liquid between the dust ring and main body of the core—just inside the sprocket on the back side. Give the Liquid Wrench a few minutes to work through the bearings. Spin the freewheel several times and move it to a dry piece of paper, then flush again. If the ball bearings inside the core are dirty, the first newspaper will be dark with grime. A third flushing may be necessary. Allow the bearings to dry for a few minutes, then apply a fine, light bicycle oil.

Spoke Replacement and Wheel Truing

Look closely at an individual spoke. You will see a long shank with threads at the top where it screws into the nipple (protruding through the rim hole and holding the spoke in place and under desired tension), and at the other end a right-angle crook that holds it in the hub. That sharp bend is the danger point, the place where when stress becomes too great, life ends. It's curtains for the spoke, curses for the rider, and an opportunity for the spoke wrench to see daylight once again.

More common, however, is a spoke that simply needs adjustment to help realign (make "true" again) a wheel. Wheels can be out of true in two ways: they can sway from side to side, and they can have high and low spots, which is referred to as being "out of round." Study your wheel. Notice that the spokes reach out to the rim from both sides of the hub. Focus upon one spoke and think what tightening (shortening the length of) that single spoke will do. The rim will be pulled in two directions at the same time when the spoke is tightened, or moved back in two directions if loosened. Tighten the spoke and the rim will be: 1. very slightly pulled closer to the hub; and 2. to a far greater degree pulled in the direction of the side of the hub to which the other end of the spoke is attached. Loosen the spoke and the opposite movement will occur. Tighten a spoke that comes from the other side of the hub and the rim will move in that direction.

"Trueing" a wheel is most quickly and successfully accomplished with the wheel off the bike, the tire, tube, and rim tape (the actual tape or rubber sheath that lies directly over the spoke-nipple heads protruding through the rim) removed, and with the assistance of a trueing stand. Such stands have small movable metal indicators that one slides ever closer to the rim from both sides as the spoke adjustments bring the wheel increasingly into alignment. This can also be done without a stand, by using the bike itself to hold the wheel and one's thumb in place of the metal slides, and for that matter without removing anything from the wheel. Again, however, your alignment will probably not be as exact.

So, you've broken a spoke on the rear wheel and, if away from a tune-up stand, have flipped your bike on its back to remove wheel, tire, tube, and rim tape, and the freewheel as well if the spoke break is on the freewheel side. Put the wheel back on the bike without tightening axle nuts or the quick-release. (The spoke can be replaced with the

Rear wheel hub with broken spoke.

wheel off the bike, but I find it much easier when the wheel is back in place.)

Remove the broken spoke. This is very easy, for spokes usually break at the bevel and can then be unscrewed from the nipple end.

Remove the nipple from the new spoke. (You won't need it if the new spoke is exactly the same gauge—thickness—as the old, and if the old nipple's threads have not been damaged.) Look at the rear hub, concentrating on the next-closest spokes to the one that broke. If you are looking at two spoke heads next to the empty hole in the hub, you know that your new spoke must enter from the other side, to follow the alternating pattern of spoke insertion into the hub around its perimeter. Guide the spoke into the hole. (Don't be afraid to bend the spoke a bit.) Once it is completely through, look at the next-closest spoke that enters the hub in the same direction as your replacement spoke. This will be your guide to lacing your replacement—how many spokes you must cross, and which to go over or under with the new spoke. (You'll have to bend the spoke even more here; be sure to bend it along its

*New spoke being inserted
into vacant spoke hole
of rear wheel hub.*

entire length, thereby not putting a crimp in it.)

Thread the new spoke into the old or new nipple. Tighten the spoke (with the spoke wrench) until it is approximately the same tension as the rest, and then—following the procedure to be discussed—align the wheel.

The removal of tire, tube, and rim tape exposes the slotted head of the spoke nipples. The slot allows you to begin tightening or loosening each spoke with a screwdriver, though you'll need a small channel locks or preferably a vise grips to obtain sufficient tension if you've rounded the flat side of the lower nipple portion with a spoke wrench. Rim tape removal also allows you to see if too much spoke extends through the nipple head, in which case a metal file blade (I use the one on my Swiss Army knife when on tour) can be used to shorten it. (If you've purchased spare spokes of the proper length you won't be troubled by protrusion.) Restore your freewheel to its proper location and replace your wheel in the frame (if it isn't there already), as it will be when you ride. Tighten axle nuts or close the q-r lever, but keep the brakes free.

Standing behind your wheel, with the bike still on its back (or right side up if on a tune-up stand), spin the wheel with your hand and note the "wobble"—movement from side to side.

Determine the extent of the wobble by placing your thumb next to the rim (with the palm of your hand resting on the chainstay) so that your thumbnail lightly touches the rim at every point except for the wobble. At that point the rim will reach out and smack your thumbnail, or move away from it sharply; your job is to pull that wobble back into line with the rest of the rim.

Check the tension of the spokes in the area of the wobble. Do this by taking hold of each spoke roughly halfway down its length and moving it back and forth—easily. Chances are they'll be a bit more loose than the rest of the spokes in the wheel. Tighten the spoke at the center of the wobble—just a bit at a time, watching its effect upon the rim—then

Spoke wrench on spoke.

Brad standing behind wheel with spoke wrench in hand.

move on to the spokes on either side. Read the next two paragraphs before proceeding.

But how much do you tighten a spoke? And what if two spokes appear to sit smack in the middle of the problem area? Easy. Just recall that spokes reach out to the rim from both sides of the hub. Naturally, tightening a spoke coming from the right side pulls the rim toward the right; from the left hub side, to the left. If your wobble is to the right, you'll be tightening the spokes that come from the left side of your hub, and vice versa. I always start off with a slight adjustment—about a half-turn for the spoke at wobble center, one-quarter turn for spokes on either side, one-eighth turn for the next two spokes.

On occasion you might have to loosen some spokes and tighten others in the wobble area to produce a true wheel, especially if you have trued your wheel several times before. In loosening spokes follow the same pattern as above: more toward wobble center, less thereafter.

When your thumbnail-guide (Brad and Ken prefer to eyeball off the brake pads) tells you all is well, you have two final things to do. First, check your spokes for approximately the same tension on all. That is, as far as is possible to tell, *and* if working on a rear wheel, all spokes should be of one equal tension on one side of the hub, and of another equal tension amount on the other hub side; you will recall that rear-wheel freewheel-side spokes hold greater tension than those on the nonfreewheel side. You won't be perfect on this (unless you've gone all out and purchased a spoke tensionometer), but at least be close or you'll be aligning your wheel again real soon. Second, step to the side of your bike, spin the wheel, and check for its "round." If you have one high spot, tighten the spokes slightly in this area to pull the rim toward the hub a bit. But be sure to watch that you don't lose your side-to-side true as you do.

Let me add that I find wheel alignment to be the most delicate, and thus the most difficult, repair on a bike. Go easy at first, and try to be patient. Your spokes will appreciate it.

Oh, and a final word from the mechanics on this procedure. The *best* method of determining proper spoke length is to take the wheel and old spoke into a bike shop. Short of that, you can get pretty close by measuring very carefully. And ask at a bike shop if they have any old junker wheels on which you can get the hang of truing. If not, it is suggested (by our two gurus) that you pop the twenty bucks or so required to purchase a cheap steel wheel with which to practice. Think of it as tuition.

BEARING MAINTENANCE

Tools required:

6-INCH CRESCENT (to remove wheels if not quick-release)

TOOLS NECESSARY TO REMOVE FREEWHEEL (see preceding discussion)

CONE WRENCHES (whatever size required to fit your wheels)

KNIFEBLADE (or a screwdriver with very thin and sharp tip) to remove O-ring seals

SPECIAL EXTRACTOR TOOLS if you have truly sealed bearing hubs

It is important for all ATB owners to understand that there is, or rather can be, a cost to riding one's bike through water. Yes, these bikes can handle many stream crossings and commuting seasons of snow and rain before any problems become noticeable. But in the meantime, water—and the almost microscopic dirt and road grime borne along—will attack your bearings and bearing cups (races). Bearings are inexpensive and are easily replaced. But foul a race and you're suddenly talking real money.

I know. You're thinking it isn't fair, that you were told your bike's bearings were sealed against the elements. Well, for most of us not riding with the more-expensive *truly* sealed hubs, a better (and far more descriptive and true) word would be that they are *shielded;* you know, the difference between waterproof and water-*resistant*. But don't despair. As you will soon learn, the requisite (if you ride a great deal) twice-annual bearing maintenance will protect your investment, and isn't nearly the time-consuming pain you would expect.

We are still discussing wheels, and therefore wheel bearings, but once bearing service of any kind is mastered you will find all such work a great deal easier to handle.

First, remove your rear wheel (we'll remain true to our treatment of the more difficult; front wheels are a comparative snap). Remove also the freewheel and quick-release skewer. Now, if you are one of the relatively few riders who has truly sealed bearings (small, round metal cartridges) you must remove the lock nut, cone-shaped sleeve nut and washer, and finally the axle itself. (See *Specialized* sheet for instructions.) Then, using the bearing puller (Tool A on the sheet) remove the sealed bearing, with a cloth wipe the inside of the hub clean, apply a slight film of oil on the new bearing, and install it in the hub. Do the same on the other side; replace the axle and all cones, nuts, and washers; and then adjust bearing pressure according to the directions provided below for nonsealed hubs. Realize, however, that the added cost of sealed hubs should buy you peace of mind and save you a good deal of maintenance. Brad rides with such hubs, has four thousand miles on them, and finds them still smooth as glass.

Like most of us, I ride with "shielded"—not sealed—bearings, in which a tight-fitting rubber O-ring replaces the very pervious metal dustcap of old. Lying within the hub housing and directly over the bearings, the O-rings do a very good job of keeping most water and grit from making a home in my hubs.

Twice a year, however, I break down the wheels as described above (except for the difference of leaving the axle in place), and with a sharp

This hub has been extensively engineered to serve you better and offers many new features.

1. An improved aerodynamic shape.

2. Spoke holes are carefully shaped to provide optimal support for the spoke at its elbow.

3. Shielded, sealed bearings provide:

a) Lower roffing resistance because of low friction seals, non-contact shields, and precision ground and polished races.

b) Low maintenance, because the bearings are BOTH sealed and shielded; dirt cannot penetrate.

4. The duraluminum anodized body is corrosion and stain proof.

SERVICE NOTES

It is important to avoid exposing the hub to volatile solvents or penetrating oils (gasoline, kerosene, mineral spirits, acetone, WD-40, LPS-1, etc.). Simply wipe the hub when it becomes soiled. In the case of bearing roughness or failure, the hub can be easily adjusted or disassembled and worn parts replaced.

BEARING REMOVAL

a) Remove freewheel if rear hub is being worked on.

b) Loosen axle nuts with 13 & 17 mm cone wrenches. Remove outer nut and sleeve nut with chrome cover.

c) Push axle out. (You might need to tap lightly with a plastic mallet.)

d) Place bearing puller (TOOL A) into center of bearing to be removed (see ILLUS. 1).

e) Place axle into hub on the opposite side as TOOL A.

f) Tap lightly on axle with plastic mallet until bearing is removed (see ILLUS. 2).

g) Clean all particles and grease out of hub.

BEARING ASSEMBLY

a) Insert new bearing(s) into the hub.

Place bearing insert washer (TOOL B) on the axle and slip into the new bearing. Slip other bearing insert washer on the other side of the axle. Then screw the sleeve nut all the way in (see ILLUS. 3). Tighten this nut until the bearing(s) goes all the way in and seats. Remove sleeve nut and push axle out.

b) Remove both washers (TOOL B). Place axle back into hub and screw sleeve nut (with chrome washer) into the bearing. Tighten nut sufficiently to eliminate side play. Don't overtighten this, as it may damage bearing. Tighten lock nut using the cone wrenches. Check axle for smoothness.

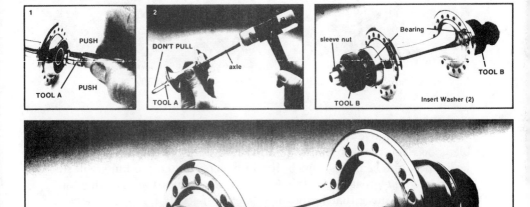

Specialized Sealed Bearing Hub

Courtesy of Specialized

Knife blade beneath rear wheel seal.   *Bearings inside rear wheel hub.*

knife blade remove the O-ring. This can be done by inserting the knife blade between the hub housing and O-ring outer lip. Pry it up and you will expose the bearings, which, if you haven't waited too long, will still be covered in grease. (By the way, our mechanics told me that one should not assume that brand new bikes, especially the less expensive models, are adequately lubed for months and months of hard use.)

After counting the bearings and noticing the slight space between them when in place in the cup, remove the bearings and wipe them, and the bearing cup or race (the inside of the hub where the ball bearings roll about, or where the "ball retainer ring," an open sleeve containing the bearings, sits), completely clean. Inspect the bearings and races (actually *race*, singular, because you will be doing one wheel side at a time) for pitting, cracking or scoring—any rough marking on the metal that can be seen by the eye and felt when you touch it. All surfaces should feel perfectly smooth. Replace worn bearings and take your wheel to a good bike shop for repair or replacement if the cups are also worn.

This must of course be done on both sides, and one can simply back off all nuts, washers, and cones (the threaded, cone-shaped pieces named for the tapering end that rests against the bearings; the other end is squared off to fit the wrench used to adjust pressure against the bearings) from both sides of the axle at the same time, or one at a time. Personally, I would never strip both sides at the same time, for this requires careful restoration to be sure that all is located properly again on the axle. In fact, my lazy approach is to remove the nuts, washers, and cones from one side of the axle only, then pull the axle free of the hub and clean both hub sides at once. When I am finished I reinsert the axle, attach the necessary pieces, and thus must adjust cone bearing pressure on one side only.

Cones; left one shows damage.

But let's return to the point of clean bearings and races, where we're about to rebuild. Apply a generous bead of fresh grease to one bearing cup. Replace the bearings, then cover them with a second bead of grease. Replace the seal by laying it in place, then tap lightly with the handle of your screwdriver or crescent wrench. (Be sure the fit is exact.) Take the axle, which in my personal maintenance method still has the cone, washer, and nut on one side, and insert it into the hub side in which you have just replaced the bearings. Be sure you have cleaned and checked the cones as well for cracks or pitting, for they too are far less expensive to replace than an entire hub. Now you can turn your wheel over and replace the bearings in the other side, for the seal and cone will keep the bearings on the reverse side from falling out.

Once the bearings are in place around the axle on this second side, replace the seal, then thread the cone into place against the bearings— but only finger-tight. Slide on the lockwasher and screw on the lock nut. Your hub is now rebuilt but not ready to be ridden, for the cones have not been adjusted to the proper pressure against the bearings. Too loose, and the wheel will roll from side to side, in time ruining your bearings and cup and cone. Too tight, and the wheel will not roll easily, also damaging the affected components.

Use the cone wrench to back off the cones a quarter turn or less if, when you turn the axle, it does not revolve easily in the hub. (The wheel is still off the bike; you should be checking its revolution by hand.) What usually happens is that a person will back off the cones too far, creating side-play. This is when the axle moves back and forth (side to side) in the hub. Even a slight amount of movement will be greatly accentuated when the wheel is replaced on the frame, so try to remove the side-play while still retaining free rolling movement of the axle.

Cone wrenches on cones.

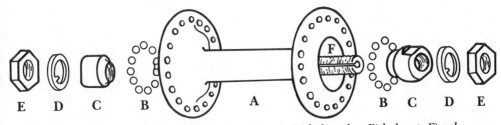

Front wheel hub. A) hub body B) bearings C) cone D) lock washer E) lock nut F) axle

Just when you think you've got the best of both worlds, tighten the lock nuts on both sides. (Hold one side fast with a crescent wrench while tightening the other side.) The first time you do this you will notice that you have tightened the cone somewhat by snugging the lock nuts—and you'll have to readjust the cone once more. Merely hold the lock nut on one side of the axle with your crescent wrench while backing off the same-side cone ever so slightly with the cone wrench. This is usually sufficient to align it properly, but if not, back off the lock nut a quarter-turn and try again. Expect it to be difficult at first, and much easier the second time.

When side-play is absent and the axle moves freely, replace the axle washers and nuts (or quick-release mechanism) and freewheel, and restore the wheel to the frame. Once it is secured, spin the wheel and check again for rolling ease and for side-play. You will find that a q-r lever tightens things up on the bearings slightly when closed, so, when adjusting the cones, leave these wheels a wee bit more loose than solid (non-quick-release) axles.

3

DERAILLEURS

Like most riders in their early forties, I grew up on a one-speed. By the time of my first cross-country tour, in 1965, I was the proud owner of a "twist-grip" three-speed—the kind that housed its extremely complicated and mysterious transmission system inside a fat rear-wheel hub. A week before the ride, thinking I should know my bike completely before hitting the road, I managed to remove the housing cover. As I wrote in my first book many years ago, inside sat a jeweler's paradise of springs and gears. It was exactly as it had been when I first faced long division—the sweaty palms and hollow stomach that accompanied the unfortunately correct instinctual knowledge that I had met a challenge far beyond me.

Ah, but then came derailleurs. Difficult for my young Midwest mouth to pronounce, they were anything *but* difficult to master. Unlike three-speeds, the entire transmission was open to view, and in an hour of study I learned to work the simple, obvious-in-purpose high- and low-gear adjusting screws.

Since then derailleurs have improved greatly in performance, been "sealed" amazingly well to the elements, and remain—even with the addition recently of "click" shifting—wonderfully simple to adjust. And yet many, many recreational riders are too fearful to approach their changers (an old term for derailleurs) with a screwdriver. Too bad.

But it needn't be so. The following pages and pictures are designed first to provide an understanding of these excellent mechanisms, and next to embolden you to take them in hand. An hour is all that's re-

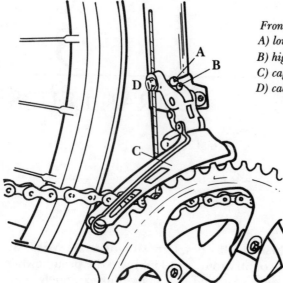

Front derailleur.
A) low gear adjusting screw
B) high gear adjusting screw
C) cage
D) cable anchor bolt

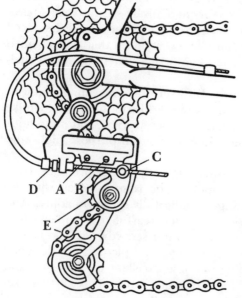

Rear derailleur.
A) low gear adjusting screw
B) high gear adjusting screw
C) cable anchor bolt
D) adjusting barrel
E) pulleys

quired to make sloppy shifting, and fear of transmission breakdown, a thing of the past.

OPERATION

Derailleur in French means "to take from the rails"; in cycling it refers to the movement of one's chain from one sprocket to another. This is accomplished through a series of shifters, gear cables, and front and rear derailleurs.

Basically, a gear cable runs from the shifter (also called shift lever, shift handle, or gear handle) along the down tube and chainstay, through a cable-adjusting barrel (similar in principle to that found on brakes), to a cable clamp bolt on the changer. When you push forward on a mountain bike's thumb shifter you tighten the cable, which causes the derailleur to lift the chain from a smaller sprocket and set it upon a larger one. Naturally, there are limits to how far in either direction you would wish your chain to go; this limitation is established by "high" and "low" gear adjusting screws. The high gear screw on rear derailleurs keeps the chain from moving beyond the smallest sprocket and falling off the freewheel; the low gear screw keeps the chain from moving beyond the largest sprocket and attacking your spokes. The third screw present on some changers is an "angle" screw. Its task is to move the derailleur body so that the upper (tension) pulley is at an optimum position below the freewheel for transporting the chain.

Below the derailleur housing are two pulleys, or rollers. Notice that the chain rolls over one and under the second. The top pulley is the "jockey" or "guide" pulley—named for its job of jockeying the chain into place over a sprocket. The bottom one is the "tension" pulley, for it takes up the slack in the chain when the derailleur moves from a larger to a smaller sprocket. The final thing you should notice are the points of lubrication (seen now only in older, nonsealed changers)—small holes in the derailleur body that run toward the internal springs. If these springs can be seen, apply a couple drops of lubricant (petroleum base if most of your riding is on pavement; nonpetroleum base if your bike is often in dirt or sand) each month, and wipe off the excess.

DERAILLEUR ADJUSTMENT

Tools required:

SMALL SCREWDRIVER

SMALL CRESCENT (perhaps)

NEEDLE-NOSE PLIERS (perhaps)

Before doing anything, give your bike a thorough visual inspection, for the most common "adjustment" problems on ATBs are bent derailleurs, bent derailleur hangers (a "hanger" is the metal plate that attaches the changer to the bike), and stretched cables. If none of these obvious difficulties are present, you will have to move on to the more delicate procedures.

If you have purchased your bike in the past three years, there is a good chance that it is outfitted with either of the two major "click" shifting systems: SunTour "AccuShift" or Shimano "SIS" (Shimano Index System). Because both companies have kindly allowed us to reprint their adjustment instructions, and because these instructions are so clear and to the point, I will let their words stand as all that is necessary for you click shifters. After that, however, I will add the required paragraphs for those of us still stuck in friction mode. Everyone, I think, might benefit in overall understanding of their components by reading this section in its entirety.

And now for those of us with old-style derailleurs. By far the most frequent "transmission" problem encountered by cyclists can be solved with a few slight turns of the high- and low-gear adjusting screws. Let's say your chain can't quite make it up onto the largest sprockets of the freewheel. Recalling that the larger freewheel sprockets provide the lower (easier to pedal) gears, simply turn counterclockwise the "L" screw of the rear derailleur—a quarter- or half-turn to start. If your chain falls off the smallest sprocket (highest gear) of your freewheel, turn the "H" screw on the rear derailleur clockwise—thereby limiting the chain's movement away from the freewheel.

Similar problems with the chainrings in front can be solved through the adjustment of the front derailleur limiting screws. Look closely inside the derailleur housing and, with some, you will be able actually to see these limiting screws making contact with the body.

Let's return to the problem of the chain not quite reaching up onto the largest freewheel sprocket. You've adjusted the "L" screw, can in fact see that the housing is not making contact with the limiting screw, and yet the chain can't quite fall into place. In such a case (very infrequent) the problem is not with the derailleur, but with the cable. It has stretched over time, and now must be readjusted. Most recent bikes have gear-cable adjustment barrels to remove this slack quickly and

Use the following procedure to make the adjustment of SIS:

1. Pre-stretch cable
Connect the inner cable with the rear derailleur and pull on it as shown here in order to eliminate the initial stretching.

2. Top and Low stroke adjustment
I) SIS—»Friction system (refer to chart A: change the mode to "Friction system", and then fold the ring back down to engage the locking mechanism.)

II) Adjust the stroke, as seen below

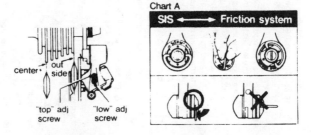

center · out side

"top" adj screw   "low" adj screw

Chart A

SIS ◄────► Friction system

3. Adjustment of the inner cable tension
I) Friction system—»SIS (fold down the ring, as shown in Chart A)

II) Operate the shifting lever to shift the chain from the top gear to the 2nd gear. If the chain will *not move to the 2nd gear,* turn the cable adjusting barrel to increase the tension — 1. (counter clockwise). If it moves past the 2nd gear, decrease the tension — 2. (clockwise).

III) Next, with the chain on the 2nd gear, increase the inner cable tension while turning the crank forward. Stop turning the cable adjusting barrel *just before the chain makes noise against the 3rd gear.* This completes the adjustment.

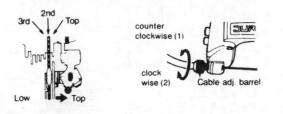

3rd   2nd   Top

Low   Top

counter clockwise (1)

clock wise (2)   Cable adj. barrel

NOTE: Derailleur will shift toward top gear if shifting mode is switched while pedaling.

SunTour AccuShift Setup Instructions

1. Check the inner and outer stroke limit to make sure that the guide pulley lines up precisely under the smallest freewheel cog at the high limit, and the largest cog at the low limit of the stroke (refer to Figure 1). Make any necessary adjustments.

2. Shift the chain on to the largest freewheel cog and pre-stretch the cable by pulling back firmly on the right shift lever. Remove any cable slack.

3. Check the derailleur angle. The body assembly should be parallel to the chainstay. Adjust with the angle adjusting screw if necessary.

4. The chain length is correct when, with the bike in *top gear*, the dot on the outer cage falls between the two marks on the plastic cage pivot bushing (refer to Figure 2). (NOTE: on a 3000 derailleur, the cage pivot stop pin should line up with the notch in the cage pivot bracket). Shift.

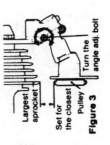

Largest sprocket
Smallest sprocket
Pulley

Figure 1

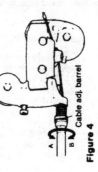

Cage
Dot
Markings

Figure 2

Courtesy of SunTour

5. Shift the chain into *lowest gear*. Make sure that the guide pulley is as close to the largest freewheel cog as possible, without touching it (refer to Figure 3). Adjust with the angle adjusting screw.

6. Shift the chain to the outboard cog. If the chain hesitates coming off the largest cog, increase the distance between the guide pulley and the largest sprocket by a small increment.

7. Shift one stop in from the outboard cog. If the shift to the second cog is not smooth, or the chain grinds, take one of the following steps (refer to Figure 4):

   a. If the chain does not move far enough to smoothly engage the second sprocket (undershift), gradually turn the cable adjusting barrel counterclockwise until it shifts, then turn back ¼ to ½ turn.

   b. If the chain moves too far (overshift), gradually turn the cable adjusting barrel clockwise until you have smooth shifting.

8. Shift back and forth several times to check for over- or under-shifting. Adjust the limit screws if necessary.

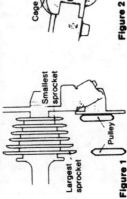

Largest sprocket
Set for the closest Pulley
turn the angle adj. bolt

Figure 3

A
B Cable adj. barrel

Figure 4

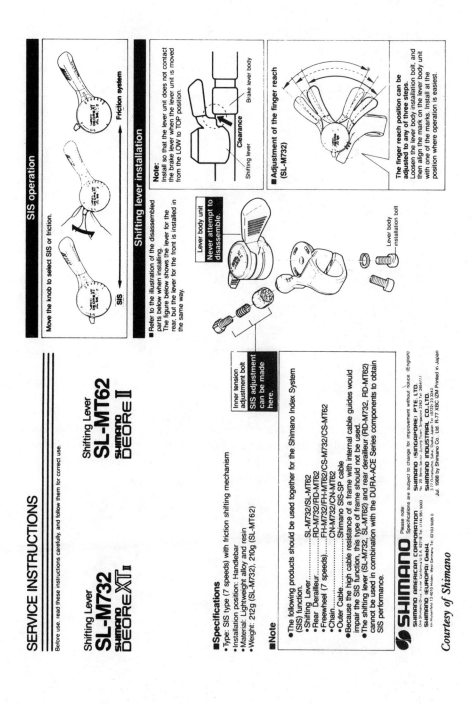

SERVICE INSTRUCTIONS

Before use, read these instructions carefully, and follow them for correct use.

Shifting Lever
SL-M732
SHIMANO DEORE XT II

Shifting Lever
SL-MT62
SHIMANO DEORE II

■Specifications
- Type: SIS type (7 speeds) with friction shifting mechanism
- Installation position: Handlebar
- Material: Lightweight alloy and resin
- Weight: 212g (SL-M732), 210g (SL-MT62)

■Note
- The following products should be used together for the Shimano Index System (SIS) function.
  - Shifting Lever....................SL-M732/SL-MT62
  - Rear Derailleur..................RD-M732/RD-MT62
  - Freewheel (7 speeds)......FH-M732/FH-MT62/CS-M732/CS-MT62
  - Chain..................................CN-M732/CN-MT62
  - Outer Cable.......................Shimano SIS-SP cable
- Because the high cable resistance of a frame with internal cable guides would impair the SIS function, this type of frame should not be used.
- The shifting lever (SL-M732, SL-MT62) and rear derailleur (RD-M732, RD-MT62) cannot be used in combination with the DURA-ACE Series components to obtain SIS performance.

SHIMANO AMERICAN CORPORATION One Shimano Drive, Irvine, California U.S.A. 92718 Tel. (714) 951-5003

SHIMANO (SINGAPORE) PTE. LTD. No. 20 Benoi Sector, Jurong Town, Singapore 2262 Tel. 2654777

SHIMANO INDUSTRIAL CO., LTD. 77 Oimatsucho, Sakai, Osaka, Japan Tel. (0722) 23 3243

SHIMANO (EUROPA) GmbH. Im Hasenfeld 13 4010 Hilden, West Germany Tel. 02103 5605 0

Please note: Specifications are subject to change for improvement without notice. (English)

Jul. 1988 by Shimano Co., Ltd. R-77 XBC IZM Printed in Japan

Courtesy of Shimano

SIS operation

Move the knob to select SIS or friction.

SIS

Friction system

Shifting lever installation

- Refer to the illustration of the disassembled parts below when installing. The figure below shows the lever for the rear, but the lever for the front is installed in the same way.

Lever body unit
Never attempt to disassemble.

Inner tension adjustment bolt

SIS adjustment can be made here.

Lever body installation bolt

Note:
Install so that the lever unit does not contact the brake lever when the lever unit is moved from the LOW to TOP position.

Clearance

Shifting lever

Brake lever body

■Adjustment of the finger reach (SL-M732)

The finger reach position can be adjusted to any of three steps. Loosen the lever body installation bolt, and then align the mark on the lever body unit with one of the marks. Install at the position where operation is easiest.

Model : SL-XDOO-CH

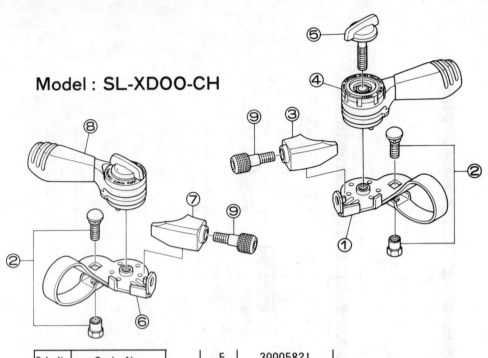

Refer No.	Code No.
1	31550205
2	31065521
3	31553201
4	31579121

5	30005821
6	31550206
7	31553202
8	31579141
9	31572301

Courtesy of SunTour

easily (as with the brake-cable adjustment systems); if yours does not, shift onto the smallest freewheel sprocket, then loosen the "cable fixing (or anchor) bolt" (which clamps the cable into place on the derailleur housing), shorten the cable slightly, and then tighten the anchor bolt again.

CABLE REPLACEMENT

Tools required:

SMALL SCREWDRIVER

SMALL CRESCENT

NEEDLE-NOSE PLIERS

Back when all my riding was done on thin-tire touring bikes, I broke, on average, one or two derailleur cables a year. These were, of course, rear cables, for rear derailleurs see so much more use than do front changers. These days, however, when by far the majority of my roughly ten thousand annual miles are put on mountain bikes, I can still say I've never, ever broken a cable front or rear.

You'll understand why when you compare bikes; ATB cables look like they belong on motorcycles. Our mechanics informed me that when they do see mountain-bike cable breaks they are, generally, the result of one of two problems: 1. the cable-fixing bolt has chewed up the cable and individual metal strands begin breaking or fraying backwards (see photo); or 2. moisture creates rust in a portion of the cable housing (the black or other-color plastic sheath inside which the metal cable runs) and jams cable movement.

Very rarely do ATB cables break at the shift lever, as they do on road bikes. But there is one great similarity, one that has required me to replace cables on both thin- and fat-tire bikes, though not because of

Rear derailleur cable fray.

breaks. This is my occasional failure to crimp an "end cap" (the tiny metal sleeve that slips over the cut end of a cable to prevent it from fraying) sufficiently to hold it in place. When it comes time to remove the cable for lubrication (usually twice a year, when I'm servicing my bearings), the fraying prevents me from pushing it through the housing once again, and a complete replacement is required.

Begin this process by loosening the cable-fixing bolt of whichever derailleur is affected by the broken cable. Remove the cable—but only after taking careful note of the cable position on its final path around the derailleur housing "blocks" to the fixing bolt. If the rear derailleur is involved, screw the cable-adjusting barrel clockwise—into the derailleur body—until it stops, but only on a nonindex system. If your nonindex thumb shifter has a brakelike cable-adjusting barrel on it (similar to that found near the derailleur body), screw it until it is flush with the shifter body. Place the lever in its most relaxed (no tension being applied to the cable) position. Feed the noncylinder end of the new cable through the cable housing (I've always used grease or oil when doing this; the mechanics told me they prefer to spray Tri-Flow

Cable end protruding from shift lever.

into the housing, and that Shimano recommends using no oil what-soever inside the housing on their index-shift bikes), then through the cable-adjusting barrel (if present) and on to the cable-fixing bolt. *Note:* Some mountain bike shift levers require that they be pushed forward a bit to allow a proper angle for cable insertion through the thumb-shifter housing.

When replacing a rear derailleur cable, pull the cable slightly taut (not so much that the derailleur body moves) and secure it by tighten-ing the cable-fixing bolt, but only after stretching it somewhat (as indi-cated on the instruction sheets). The rear derailleur pulleys should be in line with the smallest freewheel sprocket at this point. If they are not, turn the high-gear adjusting screw until that line is attained; if it cannot be reached with the adjusting screw, it means you have pulled the cable too tight. Loosen the cable-fixing bolt and readjust the cable tension.

To make the low gear adjustment, first be sure that cable stretch is not the reason for the derailleur's failure to reach the largest sprockets. If this is not the problem, carefully shift the chain onto the largest freewheel sprocket; if this can't be done, turn the low-gear adjusting screw counterclockwise until it can. Then adjust the thumb shifter until the rear derailleur pulleys are in perfect line with the largest freewheel sprocket and turn the low-gear adjusting screw clockwise—into the changer body—until you feel resistance.

When replacing a front derailleur cable, loosen the cable-anchor bolt to allow for cable movement, then place the chain on the largest rear and smallest front sprockets. Then turn the low-gear adjusting screw until there's a slight clearance between the chain and the inside plate of the chain cage (chain guide). If this cannot be done it means you have pulled the cable too taut; loosen the cable-anchor bolt, correct the ten-sion, and retighten.

Next, place the chain on the smallest rear and largest front sprockets. Then turn the high-gear adjusting screw until there is a slight clearance between the chain and the outside plate of the chain cage. When these adjustments to the rear and front derailleurs have been made, switch the chain through all possible gear combinations. In each gear you should be able to position the derailleurs so that the chain does not make noise and does not rub against the metal inner and outer plates.

And a few final suggestions from Ken and Brad. In the old days, when one's derailleur was filthy, it was common to remove the entire component and swish it around in a coffee can of gasoline or other solvent. These days, however, with main pivot springs sealed, such action would hurt more than help. Also, do not use WD-40 to lubricate the inside of cable housings; it is an excellent solvent, but is far too light to be counted on for long-term lubrication.

4

BRAKES

Most components on a bike are essential to gaining and maintaining mobility. We therefore notice when their performance slackens and takes a toll on our speed. But brakes are another matter. If they stop us they're working, right? And if after a month or two of hard riding a longer time is required to stop the bike, we simply apply them a few seconds earlier. Big deal.

Unfortunately, it just could be the biggest deal of your life. Next time you're riding the flat at a fair clip, stop pedaling, mark your position exactly when passing the back end of a parked car, and count off "One thousand, two thousand . . ." You know, the way we counted seconds when playing hide-and-seek as kids. You will find that when traveling at the moderate commuting pace of, say, 10 mph, you will pass an entire automobile's length in the span of two seconds.

So what? Well, a poorly adjusted brake can easily cost you two measly seconds in coming to a halt. It doesn't seem important, *won't* seem important till you have to slam 'em on for all they're worth—for those few times when the rush-hour motorist can't be bothered with time-consuming caution, for those white-knuckle moments when too high a curb sits to the right and too big a Buick to the left and, before you, looms a sewer grating or manhole. And then there are those trail times when screaming descents in dust or loose rock requires, all of a sudden, that you break your momentum or eat an aspen.

Before it happens, therefore, take a moment to learn what can be the most important component on a bike. Remember, a last-minute flat tire can delay a weekend trail ride or, if you're commuting, cause you to catch a bus. But lousy brakes can put you *under* one.

Before we launch into the individual kinds of brakes found on ATBs, I'll offer our mechanics' words that the same kind of adjustment—rim clearance, pad alignment, toe-in—is necessary for all. The difference lies in how these are achieved. The mechanics of it is relatively simple, they say, but because we are dealing with very slight adjustments of physically small components, getting things right is often an exasperating juggling act.

You will notice again the excellent drawings and instructions provided by the component companies. These of course make my task a great deal simpler; I suggest you find the particular entry that corresponds most closely to your brake model (reading the other entries also for tips that are not repeated throughout) and follow the adjustment procedure very carefully. Because these guides are already present I asked Ken and Brad not to repeat their own step-by-step instructions, but instead to provide more general directions concentrating on what most riders miss when working on their brakes.

CANTILEVER ADJUSTMENT

Tools required:

ALLEN WRENCHES (usually a 2, 5, 6 mm)

OPEN-END WRENCH OR SMALL CRESCENT

"The real mystery of brakes, solved in a nutshell," said Ken as he and Brad gathered their instruments for surgery, "is the adjustment of spring tension to center the pads evenly off the rim."

"But mystery doesn't mean *difficult*," Brad added, and a very inexpensive bike was wheeled in for demonstration purposes. It had cantilever brakes of the *external spring* style. That is, the springs that hold the brake pads off the wheel rim were not enclosed (as with most), but instead lay open to view and wrapped around the braze-on brake stud (or "pivot boss"—the round shaft on the fork blade on which is mounted the cantilever arm).

A quick and dirty method of repair with these external-spring cantilevers, and indeed about the only thing one can do with this model

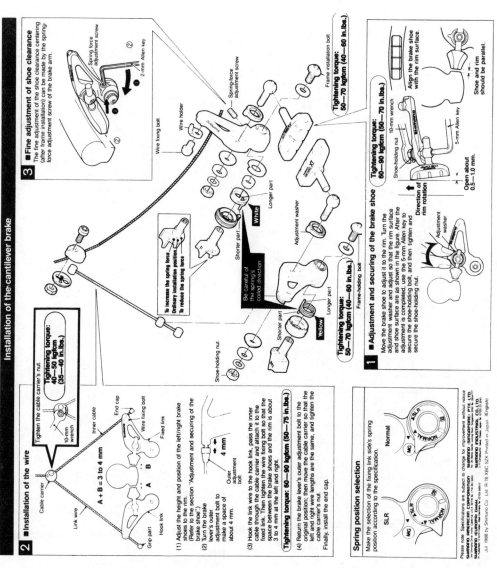

Installation of the cantilever brake

3 ■Fine adjustment of shoe clearance

The fine adjustment of the shoe clearance centering (after frame installation) can be made by the spring-force adjustment screw of the brake arm.

Spring force adjustment screw

2-mm Allen key

Frame installation bolt

Tightening torque:
50—70 kgf•cm (40—60 in.lbs.)

Spring-force adjustment screw

Wire holder

Wire fixing bolt

**Tightening torque:
60—90 kgf•cm (50—70 in.lbs.)**

Align the brake shoe with the rim surface.

Shoe and rim should be parallel.

10-mm wrench

Shoe-holding nut

5-mm Allen key

Direction of rim rotation

Open about 0.5—1.0 mm.

Adjustment washer

Longer part

White

Shorter part

Be careful of the spring's coiled direction

To increase the spring force,
Ordinary installation position.
To reduce the spring force

Adjustment washer

**Tightening torque:
50—70 kgf•cm (40—60 in.lbs.)**

Shoe-holding nut

Shorter part

Longer part

Yellow

Frame-holding bolt

**Tightening torque:
50—70 kgf•cm (40—60 in.lbs.)**

1 ■Adjustment and securing of the brake shoe

Move the brake shoe to adjust it to the rim. Turn the adjustment washer and adjust so that the rim surface and shoe surface are as shown in the figure. After the adjustment is completed, use the 5-mm Allen key to secure the shoe-holding bolt, and then tighten and secure the shoe-holding nut.

2 ■Installation of the wire

Tighten the cable carrier's nut.

10-mm wrench

End cap

Inner cable

Cable carrier

Wire fixing bolt

Fixed link

Link wire

A + B = 3 to 4 mm

A   B

Grip part

Hook link

(1) Adjust the height and position of the left/right brake shoes to the rim.
(Refer to the section "Adjustment and securing of the brake shoe".)

(2) Turn the brake lever's outer adjustment bolt to make a space of about 4 mm.

Outer adjustment bolt

4 mm

(3) Hook the link wire to the hook link, pass the inner cable through the cable carrier and attach it to the fixed link. Then tighten the wire fixing bolt so that the space between the brake shoes and the rim is about 3 to 4 mm at the left and right.

Tightening torque: 60—90 kgf•cm (50—75 in.lbs.)

(4) Return the brake lever's outer adjustment bolt to the original position; then move the cable carrier so that the left and right wire lengths are the same, and tighten the cable carrier's nut.

Finally, install the end cap.

Spring position selection

Make the selection of the fixing link side's spring position according to the specification.

SLR

MG

SLR

NORMAL

Normal

MG

SLR

NORMAL

Please note: Specifications are subject to change for improvement without notice.
SHIMANO AMERICAN CORPORATION   SHIMANO (SINGAPORE) PTE. LTD.
SHIMANO INDUSTRIAL CO., LTD.

Jul 1988 by Shimano Co. Ltd. R.78 XBC SZK Printed in Japan (English)

Courtesy of Shimano

Model : BA-XCOO

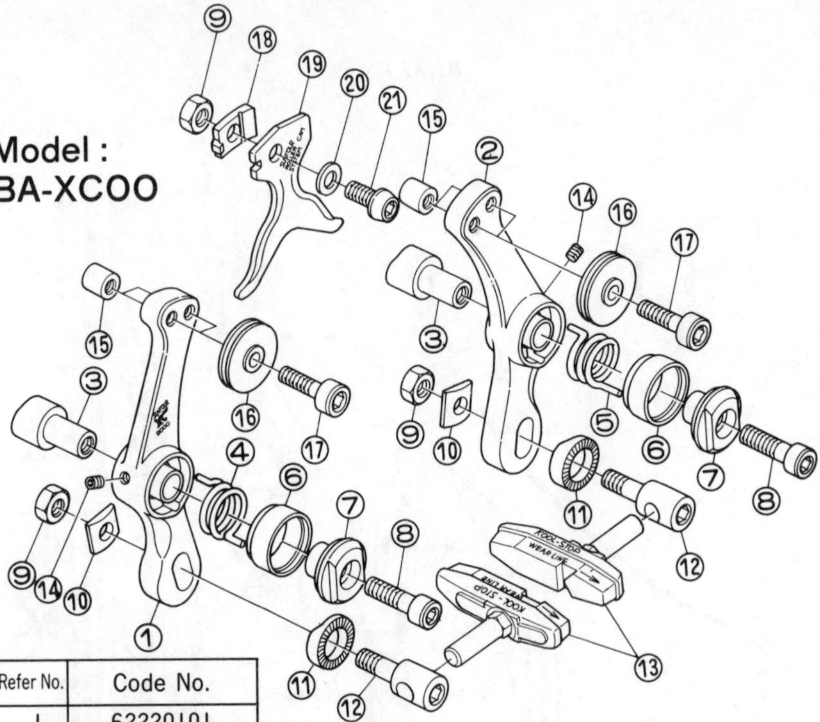

Refer No.	Code No.
1	62220101
2	62220102
3	62211503
4	62251301
5	62251302
6	62223401
7	62220601
8	62251603
9	62215211
10	62250503
11	62250403
12	62250801
13	62292601
14	60001513
15	62221801
16	62210301
17	62251703
18	62211101
19	62210211
20	62218011
21	62211001
22	59990221
23	62222001
24	62229007

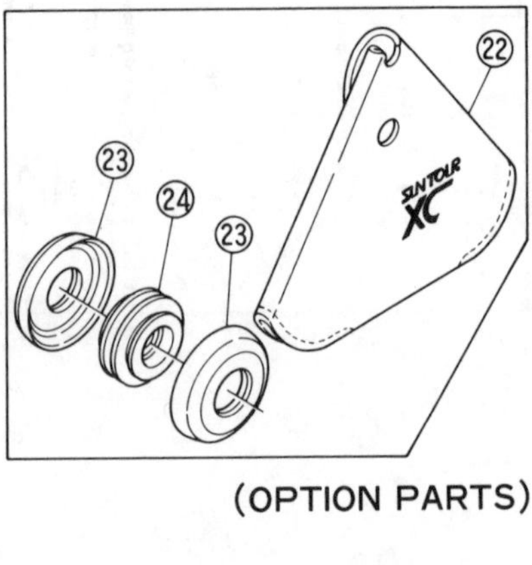

(OPTION PARTS)

Courtesy of SunTour

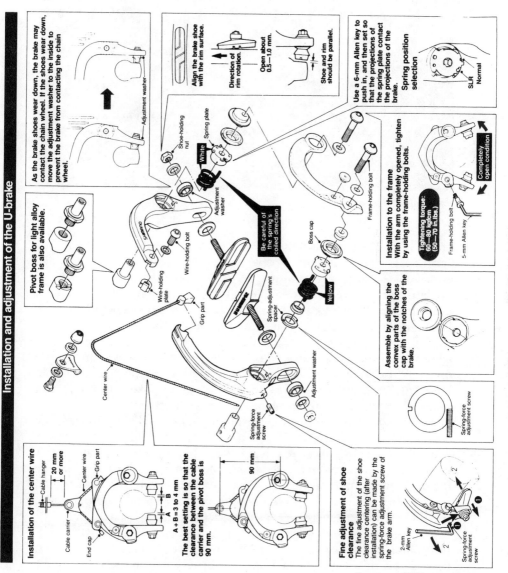

Installation and adjustment of the U-brake

As the brake shoes wear down, the brake may contact the chain wheel. If the shoes wear down, move the adjustment washer to the inside to prevent the brake from contacting the chain wheel.

Adjustment washer

Pivot boss for light alloy frame is also available.

Align the brake shoe with the rim surface.

Direction of rim rotation.

Open about 0.5—1.0 mm.

Shoe and rim should be parallel.

Use a 6-mm Allen key to push in, and then set so that the projections of the spring plate contact the projections of the brake.

Spring position selection

SLR

Normal

Shoe-holding nut

Spring plate

White

Adjustment washer

Be careful of the spring's coiled direction

Boss cap

Yellow

Wire-holding bolt

Wire-holding plate

Frame-holding bolt

Installation to the frame
With the arm completely opened, tighten by using the frame-holding bolts.

Completely open condition

Tightening torque: 60—80 kg•cm (50—70 in.lbs.)

Frame-holding bolt

5-mm Allen key

Grip part

Spring-adjustment spacer

Assemble by aligning the convex parts of the boss cap with the notches of the brake.

Adjustment washer

Center wire

Spring-force adjustment screw

Spring-force adjustment screw

Installation of the center wire

Cable hanger

20 mm or more

Center wire

Grip part

Cable carrier

End cap

A B

A + B = 3 to 4 mm

The best setting is so that the clearance between the cable carrier and the pivot boss is 90 mm.

90 mm

Fine adjustment of shoe clearance
The fine adjustment of the shoe clearance centering (after installation) can be made by the spring-force adjustment screw of the brake arm.

2-mm Allen key

Spring-force adjustment screw

Courtesy of Shimano

External-spring style cantilever.

brake, is to take hold of the transverse cable (center wire) "end part" or "grip part" (the knob on the cable end), and release it from the brake arm. Look for rust or dirt within the spring coils that might be inhibiting brake-arm movement (clean and grease if necessary). If that is not a problem take hold of each arm, one at a time, and bend them away from the rim to produce a bit more tension in the spring.

With internal springs, release the transverse cable, then use a 5-mm allen wrench (less-expensive bikes use regular bolt heads requiring an open-end or crescent) to unscrew the frame-holding bolt (the bolt that holds the brake arm to the fork). If the braze-on brake stud (the round shaft) is dry or rusted, the problem may have been located; clean it and lubricate it with grease. Notice on the Shimano cantilever drawing the enlargement of this piece. If you have never worked on your brakes you will probably—upon removing the frame-holding bolt and other pieces slowly and thoughtfully—find the coil spring inserted in the middle of three tension holes. Notice on the drawing that you should reinstall the spring in the lowest hole to reduce tension, and place it in the highest hole to increase tension.

It is a good idea, when attempting to realign spring pressure or simply pulling maintenance on your bike (regrease the brake studs twice a year if you ride a lot), to take apart and rebuild one brake arm at a time. This is because the spring coils belong on one or the other side; they are not interchangeable. It is a common mistake to replace these on the wrong studs, even though they are color coded (often brass on one side and silver on another). If they are crossed you will find that

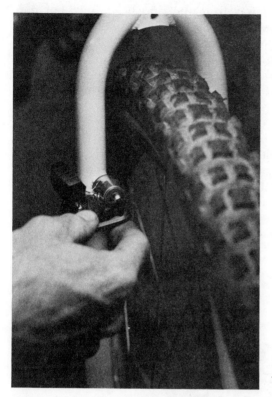

*Allen wrench in
frame-holding bolt.*

Internal-spring brake arm.

the brake arms spring out (away from the rim) beautifully, but flop ineffectually toward the rim when the brake handle is depressed. These springs in time may require replacement, and usually do so at different points in their career. When this happens take the old spring you wish replaced to the shop with you to be sure you buy the one you need.

While the brake arm is off the bike, dismantle it and clean all pieces; grease all internal pieces *except* for the ends of bolts. Brake bolts and screw ends often have a bit of thread-locking compound at the tips to hold them in place. Grease them and they will back out of their fittings. Also, when replacing the bolt, tighten it carefully and *only* until it stops. It is common for riders to give these bolts a hard twist past that point and mushroom the end of the stud, a cause of brake binding.

And now to pad alignment. Simply, the pad should strike the rim evenly top to bottom (that is, both the top and bottom portions of the pad should strike rim metal at exactly the same time), but at the upper

Internal-spring brake arm disassembled.

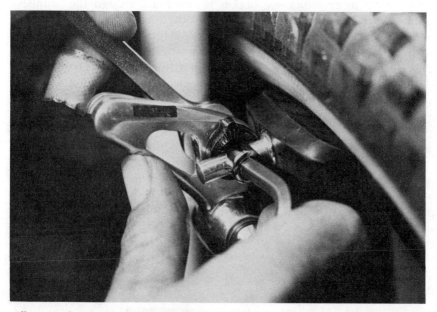

Allen wrench in brake pad adjustment.

portion of the rim. This is because the direction of cantilever brake arms cause the pads to dive down while traveling wheelward. The pad should also be aligned evenly side to side (so that the right-to-left length of the pad strikes the rim), but the front end of both the front and rear wheel pads (that portion of the pad toward the front of the bike, or in the direction of wheel movement) should be set to strike the rim before the back end of the pad does so. This is called toe-in. It helps keep the brakes from squealing and makes their performance more predictable.

Again, these alignments are described and instructions to attain them are given in the accompanying component drawings, but in general the frame-holding bolt is loosened to readjust pad alignment so that it strikes the rim squarely along its face. Gross adjustment of brake-shoe distance from the rim is achieved by loosening the brake-shoe holding bolt and nut and sliding the shoe along its shaft; fine adjustment from the rim is done with the "spring-force adjustment screw" of the brake arm (operated by a 2-mm allen).

Toe-in on more expensive brakes is obtained through the "adjustment washer" (the one with a small tab at the top, which sits above the frame-holding bolt head). On less-expensive brakes a series of conical washers (located behind the adjustment washer) must be maneuvered. This can be very difficult if attempted in a hurry, for one hand is required to operate a small screwdriver in pushing these conical washers into proper position, another required to hold the adjustment washer in place, and a third to operate the 5-mm allen or crescent to tighten all in place through the frame-holding bolt. Unfortunately most of us are one hand shy.

Brad says he usually sets up brakes with approximately two millimeters of space (roughly the thickness of a credit card folded once) between the rim and the back of the brake pad when the front of the pad is touching the rim. Also, begin adjustments with the brake-shoe stud pushed all the way into its bolt housing (away from the rim), for this will allow less flex and adjustment for pad wear later on.

Roller cam brake.

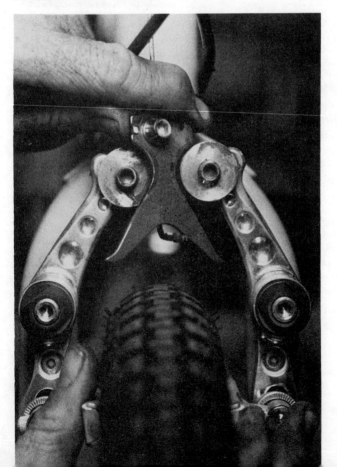

And a few words on setting up one's transverse cable (the one reaching out to both brake arms and connected to the brake handle by the brake cable). The length should be such that you obtain an even-looking triangle. Lower the cable hanger (or cable carrier; another and rather old term for this is "brake yoke") as far as possible to clear any obstructions, then adjust so that you can pinch the pads together to release the transverse cable from its home in the brake arms and thus be able to remove the wheel. If by doing this you must move the pads too far from the rim, use the brake-cable-barrel adjustor on the brake lever to provide proper clearance.

Finally, no matter what kind of brakes you have you should avoid "spaghetti cabling"—a term describing the great lengths of cable housing blousing out from some riders' handlebars on the way to their brakes. Keep them just long enough to clear the most extreme turns of the handlebars. Unnecessary inches allow cables to stretch more, thus creating the need for longer brake-response time and more frequent adjustment.

ROLLER CAM ADJUSTMENT

Tools required:

ALLEN WRENCHES (5 and 10 mm)

SUNTOUR ROLLER-WIDTH-ADJUSTMENT TOOL

A friend of mine recently took John Barnett's six-week course in bike mechanics and was kind enough to show me the hefty "Procedures Manual" he used during the class. Impressed by the overall size and approach of the manual, I glanced at it only briefly. It was in my hands long enough, however, for me to notice that it contained four full type-written sheets of instructions on the roller cam alone. Ugh.

The relatively short paragraphs that follow, even with the accompanying SunTour drawings and adjustment notes, cannot help but provide less information overall. Barnett describes these brakes as "the most demanding" of a mechanic, a sentiment held by much of the industry. But not, oddly enough, by our shop mechanics. That is, while they might agree if the overall setup and complete dismantling of roller cams is concerned, I have been assured (and know from the personal experience of riding with them for more than a year) that the adjustments and repairs required by the average mountain biker make these brakes far simpler than you fear.

We will begin with some nomenclature: the *rollers* are those round metal wheels located at the top of either brake arm; the *cam* is the double-Y-shaped metal sleeve between. It is common for bikes to be taken into a bike shop with corroded rollers impairing cam movement, or rollers that are overtightened and therefore fail to roll freely when the brake lever is depressed and the cam attempts to lift. Grooves are worn into the rollers by the cam plate over time and thus require replacement.

The first step in maintenance, adjustment, or repair of these brakes is to watch their performance when squeezing the brake lever. Notice how the rollers are moving and if the pads are striking the rim properly (read through the paragraphs on cantilever adjustment for guidance in this). Next, reach under the rim (through the spokes) and pinch the pads together; the top of the brake arms—where the rollers sit— should spread apart just enough for the cam to be twisted free.

Before you forget, reach up to the brake lever and screw the adjusting brake-lever barrel into the handle all the way. This is something that should be done no matter which kind of brake you have, for it will allow for later in-the-saddle adjustments for pad wear and cable stretch.

Look now at the braze-on brake stud. Inside is the same kind of coiled-spring setup as is present on cantilevers; the difference is that spring tension can be adjusted beyond that made possible by the three spring-tip holes present on some cantilever braze-ons. To set the proper spring tension on a roller cam, insert an allen wrench into the frame-mounting bolt, place an open-end or crescent wrench (or with some, like the old SunTour XC, a thin cone wrench) over the surrounding (around the frame-mounting bolt) beveled nut, and "dial in" the tension by holding the allen still and turning the surrounding nut (see photo).

But how much is needed? There is a tendency for people to overtighten roller-cam springs. You should search for the point at which you have the minimum amount of tension necessary to move the pads into the rim while obtaining a nice, light touch to the brake lever. Dial in a bit of tension (a minute of experimentation will show you which direction to turn the surrounding nut for greater or lesser tension), move to the other brake arm and dial in the same amount, flap the brake lever a couple times to test the feel and performance, and do micro adjustments ("tweaking" the spring tension) until all feels right.

Crescent and allen wrenches on roller cam brake.

If the cable (from the brake handle to the cam) has stretched over time, you will have to shorten it. With a 10-mm open-end or a crescent wrench and a 5-mm allen, loosen the cable-anchor clamp, pull the cable taut, and tighten once again. *Note:* The old roller models with a "stepped" cam required the use of a "roller-width-adjustment tool"—a very small bar with right angles at either end, available from SunTour or well-equipped bike shops—into the allen-headed roller bolts. This held the brake arms the proper distance apart while the other adjustments were made. Later, straight-sided cams omitted the need for this tool, but also slightly decreased optimum performance.

U-BRAKE ADJUSTMENT

Tools required:

ALLEN WRENCHES (Various sizes depending upon whether brake is Shimano or Dia Compe)

OPEN-END (various sizes) or small crescent wrench

A thorough reading of the two sections above, plus the instruction sheets from Shimano and Dia Compe, should answer almost all adjustment-related questions. I will therefore hold myself to a few short notes:

1. Proper pad placement is identical except that U-brake design requires pads to sit somewhat closer to the rim; toe-in is the same—in the direction of wheel movement (do not become confused by the under-the-bottom-bracket position of some U-brakes).

2. Brake-arm movement is the opposite of cantilevers; that is, the pads move up, toward the tire, rather than down, toward the spokes. They should therefore be set to strike the rim nearer the bottom (closer to the spokes) but still, of course, squarely across the pad face and toed-in.

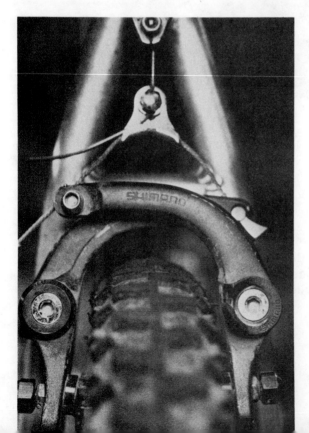

U-brake

CABLE REPLACEMENT/LUBRICATION

Tools required:

VARIOUS-SIZED ALLEN AND OPEN-END (OR CRESCENT) WRENCHES, depending upon kind of brake and manufacturer

Watch carefully as you remove the dry, worn, or broken cable from its housing and you'll learn almost all you need to know for replacement. Notice the cylinder-shaped end of the cable, held in place by the brake-handle housing. Brake cables come with one end that will fit your

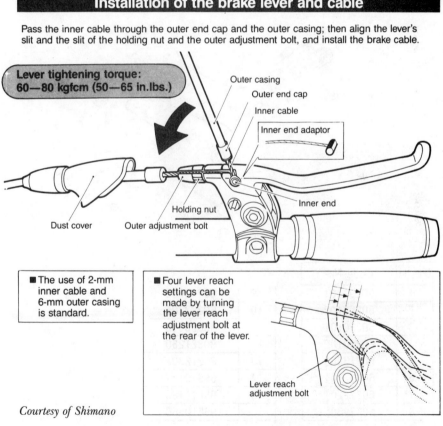

Installation of the brake lever and cable

Pass the inner cable through the outer end cap and the outer casing; then align the lever's slit and the slit of the holding nut and the outer adjustment bolt, and install the brake cable.

Lever tightening torque:
60—80 kgfcm (50—65 in.lbs.)

Outer casing
Outer end cap
Inner cable
Inner end adaptor

Dust cover
Holding nut
Outer adjustment bolt
Inner end

■ The use of 2-mm inner cable and 6-mm outer casing is standard.

■ Four lever reach settings can be made by turning the lever reach adjustment bolt at the rear of the lever.

Lever reach adjustment bolt

Courtesy of Shimano

Model : BL-XDOO

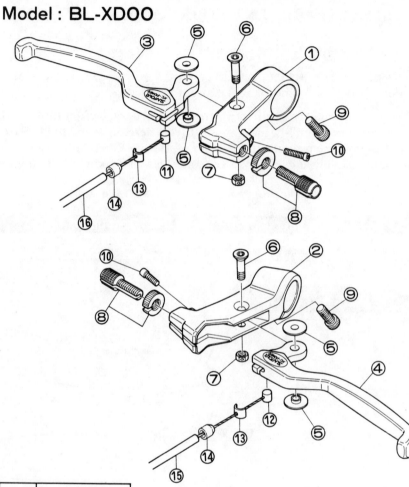

Refer No.	Code No.
1	60291101
2	60291102
3	60290101
4	60290102
5	60213005
6	60292101
7	60212201
8	60299001

9	60212605
10	60292705
11	90820680
12	90821280
13	60212801
14	59990127
15	95611160
16	95610560

Courtesy of SunTour

particular housing; the other end is to be cut off (carefully, so that the individual metal strands do not fray) to allow its placement into the cable housing and final entry into and through the cable-anchor-bolt connection.

Once having depressed the brake handle and located the cylinder end of the broken cable, remove the brake cable. Snip off the unnecessary end of the new cable, lightly grease the cable throughout its length, then insert it beneath the brake handle and into the cable housing. Run its cut end through the cable-anchor bolt, and adjust pad placement as discussed above. Excess cable can be wound into a ball or cut off.

Sometimes a crack in the cable housing, or a drop of water that manages to find its way inside, will cause brakes to "stick." Although the metal brake arms are usually suspected, and indeed the braze-on pivot bosses should be inspected for lubrication, a very likely culprit is rust inside the housing. Simply release the cable at the cable-anchor bolt, slip it completely out of its housing, grease, and reattach it. (This will be much easier if the free, cut end of the cable has been kept from fraying by a metal end cap.)

And a couple of final notes concerning all brake systems. Ken and Brad say they sometimes take sandpaper to pad surfaces when these have become too slick to grab rims properly. Rims should be cleaned occasionally with steel wool (if badly discolored with pad residue) and/or a non-oil-base liquid cleaner.

5

CHAINS

Pavement cyclists have few problems with their chains. In fact, if they can train themselves to hear the awful squeaking of a dry chain begging for lubrication and then spend five minutes applying a bit of oil (a single drop on each roller), all will be well in their drive-train world.

For mountain bikers who spend a lot of time in dirt and sand, however, it is a very different story. They *must* learn this part of their bike's anatomy, or suffer breakdowns. Occasional cleaning is a must; the kinds of lubricants available (liquid or spray petroleum bases, or non-petroleum teflons or paraffin) must be known, understood, and used.

Beyond this, mountain bikers must be able to handle broken chains in the backcountry (by adding a replacement link, or at least shorten the chain, then avoid combinations of the largest chainwheels and sprockets and thereby be able to ride home) and to free a frozen link (much more common with ATBs than with pavement bikes) when one appears.

FROZEN AND BROKEN LINKS

Tools required:

CHAIN RIVET TOOL, also called simply "chain tool"

When a link becomes frozen (a condition often caused by insufficient lubrication) it makes itself known by jumping over the teeth in the

Chain tool on chain; both rivet pins in view.

sprockets or by causing the rear derailleur to jerk forward suddenly as it passes over the jockey and tension pulleys. Elevate your rear wheel and turn the crank to find the culprit link; when you do, coat it with a light oil (if using oil as your lubrication, that is) and work the link side to side (the opposite direction of its normal movement) with your fingers. This may free it. If not, you'll have to employ the chain tool.

This tool, when viewed from the side, looks like a wide U, with two shorter "walls" of metal between. Place the tool in front of you with the handle to the right side. Twist the handle counterclockwise to remove the rivet "pin" (see photo) from view. Now, take the chain and place it over the first of these inner walls from the right side. (It will usually be somewhat wider than the left-hand wall.) Notice, when you view your chain tool from the top, that these walls have an open space in the middle and the chain roller rests in it with the "plates" on either side of the wall. (Look at an individual link. Each is made up of these metal side plates, small round bars called "rollers" to engage the teeth of the sprockets, and tiny rivets to hold the side plates and rollers together.)

To free a frozen link, place it as described above on the right-hand wall of the chain rivet tool. Turn the tool handle clockwise until the tool rivet pin touches the chain rivet. As you turn the handle more, notice how the plates move slightly farther apart. Most often only the slightest rivet adjustment is necessary to free the link. Be sure not to push the chain rivet flush with the side plate, for its length is such that it should extend slightly past the plates on both sides. If it is necessary to push the rivet flush to free the link, simply turn the chain over in the tool and apply pressure against the opposite end of the rivet.

In the case of a chain break, a spare link and chain tool in your kit

Chain tool with disconnected chain.

allows you to remove the broken link completely and replace it with a spare. This requires that the chain rivet be driven out of one side plate past the roller, yet still remain in place in the far side plate. (I *know* this sounds very confusing. But it won't be when you're attempting the repair.) Keeping the rivet in the far side plate can be a little tricky at first, so I suggest you run through this procedure a couple times before you try it on the trail. Bike shops will often have lengths of old chains with which you can practice.

Place the chain over the left-hand wall of your chain tool and turn the handle clockwise until the tool rivet pin touches the chain rivet.

Then continue turning very carefully, until the roller can be pulled free, but with the chain rivet still in the far side plate. Install the new link by turning the chain tool around and driving the chain rivet through the new roller and side plate. You'll probably find that it's frozen when replaced. If so, simply place this link on the right-hand plate and free it, following the directions above.

CLEANING AND LUBRICATION

Tools required:

CHAIN RIVET TOOL

In the past few years a number of commercial brush-and-solvent-type chain cleaners have entered the market. If used often these will do a fair job of removing the larger part of road grime. But there will come a time when the old procedure of complete chain removal, a good dunking in a coffee can of white gas (or other solvent), and a frontal attack with a toothbrush, is required. I then hang mine to drip dry, rub it with a cloth, clean all chain contact points on the bike (chainwheels, cogs, derailleur pulleys), and reinstall.

Because I am most often on dirt and pavement (relatively seldom on sand), and because I prefer a small bottle of liquid oil in my pannier to an aerosol can, I choose against both paraffin and sprays for lubrication. My practice is simply to use a single drop of oil on each roller, spin the chain a few times, let it sit for a while, then wipe almost dry with a cloth.

However, a friend of mine who rides the sands of southern Utah quite often, and another who rides primarily in dirt, swear by paraffin. Their arguments are of course a cleaner bike and "less wear and tear on the chain and all its contact points" (which they attribute to dirt not being attracted to—and held in place by—an oily, greasy chain). Yet when I asked Brad and Ken their opinions of paraffin, their response was a single word: "Dinosaur."

I begged them to expand, and heard how they tested paraffin's efficiency by adding oil to the paraffined chain of a bike they were pedaling on a tune-up stand. The cyclic rate increased dramatically. The mechanics agree that wax does not attract dirt, but teflon-base lubricants that "go to a dry rather than wet finish," they say, are almost as good at repelling dirt and sand and yet do a better job of lubrication. *And* they're much easier to apply.

My own attempts with paraffin came about a decade ago, on a thin-tire touring bike I was using for daily commutes. I cleaned the chain thoroughly, melted a block of paraffin in a coffee can on the stove (one fellow I know uses an old electric frying pan), and was sold on the idea for the first two weeks. But it was winter, and the wax broke down quickly. And because I was in graduate school there was little time to hassle with removing the chain for a second dip.

Neither of my wax-preferring friends commutes under such conditions. One simply takes the time required to make repeated dippings; the other keeps a second waxed chain in reserve. (I wish it had been with him during a recent four-day dirt retracing of Lewis and Clark's route across Idaho. By day three our chains had eaten so much dust they started creaking. I silenced mine with oil, but listened to his cry its way to camp.)

DETERMINING CHAIN LENGTH

How long should your chain be? Long enough to do the job properly. So went my question and Ken's answer, followed by a lengthy explanation (and demonstration) of why the good old days of easy determinations are gone forever.

Until only a few years ago there were two or three standard methods that seldom failed. My preference (simply because I could remember it) was the method that began with putting the chain on the largest sprockets, front and rear. This pulled the rear derailleur cage almost parallel with the chainstay. I would then give it a bit of assistance to make it taut, and try to lift the chain at the top of the chainring. If I had between one-half and one full link of extra chain at this point, I was fine.

But today, due to index shifting and other sophistications, one must determine length by "derailleur-specific directions." In other words, consult your owner's manual. Personally, I still prefer the foolproof plan of riding a bike long enough to know that all works perfectly, then very carefully counting the number of links and going with it always.

6

SADDLES AND SEATPOSTS

REMOVAL AND REPLACEMENT

Tools required:

ALLEN OR OPEN-END OR CRESCENT WRENCH, depending on kind of saddle clamp

The mechanical workings of saddles and seatposts are so self-explanatory that they scarcely require inclusion in a mechanics book. For example, a quick glance under your saddle will make evident which of the two most common types of saddle clamps you have (the old style of clamps and plates, requiring at least one crescent, or the easiest and most prevalent of all—a single allen-head bolt pointing upward) and thus which wrench you'll need. There is a third kind of saddle clamp, fortunately seldom seen these days, which requires a box- or open-end wrench to reach two bolt heads hiding beneath the saddle. Bad design, at least for adjustments.

Once you've looked at your clamp and chosen your tool, loosen the bolt, reposition the saddle, and tighten. Pretty tough.

Likewise, the quick-release lever found on almost all ATBs also makes seatpost adjustment a snap. (However, review the q-r lever cautions noted in Chapter 2.)

But there are a few other points to bring up about these simple mechanisms. For instance, Ken and Brad informed me that while all seatposts should be greased before insertion (and regreased two or

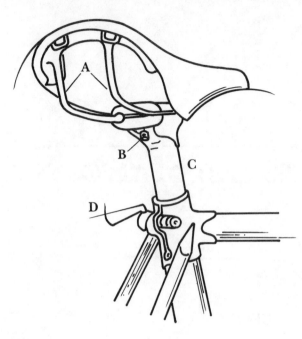

Most common saddle/seatpost.
A) rails
B) allen head adjustment bolt
C) seatpost
D) quick-release lever

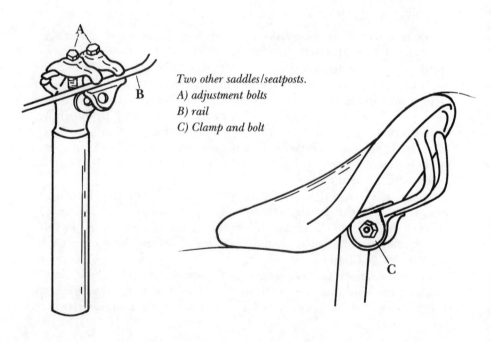

Two other saddles/seatposts.
A) adjustment bolts
B) rail
C) Clamp and bolt

three times a season if the bike is ridden often), aluminum posts *must* be well greased to prevent a permanent welding of the post to the frame. Especially (but not exclusively) true if near saltwater spray, they warn of the electro-chemical bonding that causes the aluminum and steel alloy to act like epoxy. The mechanics have been able to free some by filling the seat tube or post with dry ice. But they also have a collection of frame/post combinations that are married forever.

Other points:

1. Grease up saddle clamps as well as seatposts.

2. Pay attention to the maximum seatpost-height markings; bike shops see a lot of bent posts.

3. Just because the last joker who rode a rental left the saddle at a queer angle doesn't mean you have to put up with it. If you're renting a bike, spend a minute to adjust both saddle and post, and take your own saddle with you on vacation (if renting a bike) to insure maximum comfort.

7

HANDLEBARS AND HEADSETS

The headset is another of those most-often-neglected parts of the bike. It is abused, misunderstood, taken for granted because it seldom acts up, and roundly cursed when—after years of disregard—a rider experiences some difficulty and finds that things have rusted up inside. Imagine.

Our mechanics' warnings about the electro-chemical bonding of seatposts and frames is true for handlebar stems and headsets as well. In fact, they say it is even more apt, given that ATB seatposts are raised and lowered often, and handlebars rarely budged. So be warned, and use grease liberally.

BAR-HEIGHT ADJUSTMENT

Tools required:

ALLEN OR CRESCENT WRENCH

MALLET (or anything substantial to whack the extender bolt)

First, raising and lowering your handlebars does not involve the headset, so do not begin messing with the stack of locknuts and lockwashers immediately above your head tube. All that is involved is an expander bolt and wedge nut, an understanding of how things work in this part of the bike, and a few good wallops in the right place.

Allen wrench in extender bolt head.

Notice the expander bolt in the drawing. At the other end of this bolt—inside the head tube—is either an angle-expander nut (see photo) or a wedge nut (an "exterior" or "interior" wedge). When the expander bolt is tightened, the angled nut presses against the head-tube wall; the wedge-nut type works by drawing the nut up inside the

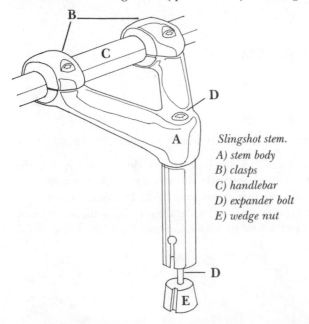

Slingshot stem.
A) stem body
B) clasps
C) handlebar
D) expander bolt
E) wedge nut

stem, forcing the stem walls out against the head tube.

Now take the second important step in all mechanical repairs: a *close* look at everything that might be affected or at all involved. In the case of lowering or raising bars, many brake assemblies are involved (through the lengthening or shortening of the brake cable). If this is so with your bars, simply disengage the brake cable until the bar is adjusted, then readjust cable length and reattach when through.

Loosen the expander bolt two or three turns. You will notice when it becomes easier to turn; try not to back it out from the bolt entirely, for you'll then have to turn your bike upside down to free the nut. If your bike is new your bars can probably be moved when the expander bolt is loosened. But if not you'll have to rap the top of the expander bolt when it is loosened but still connected to the frozen angle or wedge nut inside the head tube. Use a mallet, the backside of a crescent, or anything appropriate and nearby. You'll feel it release inside. Position the bars where you wish and retighten the expander bolt.

Mallet over extender bolt head   *External wedge.*

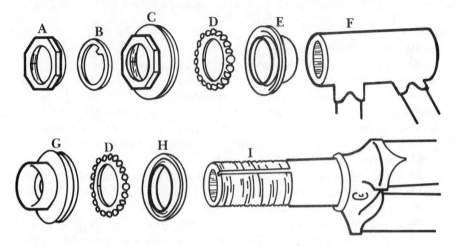

Headset. A) locknut B) lock washer C) adjusting cup/top threaded race D) bearings E) top head/set race F) head tube G) bottom head/set race H) fork crown race I) fork

BEARING MAINTENANCE

Tools required:

ALLEN WRENCH

HEADSET WRENCH OR LARGE CRESCENT

The purpose of a headset is to secure the fork to the frame, and to do so in a manner that allows free rotation of the fork (and thereby the handlebars) to the right and left. Look closely at the drawing, put on your thinking cap, quit telling yourself that only "born" mechanics can understand such things, and you'll soon see how this is performed.

Two wrenches held to headset; mechanic is not *straddling bike.*

Notice that the top of the fork is threaded. It is held in place in the head tube by the top threaded race (bearing cup). This race, and the fork crown race, are positioned with the top and bottom bearings to allow for rotation. In all my riding the greatest difficulty I've had with headsets (a slight problem in turning the bars side to side) was remedied in the following fifteen-minute repair.

First, using the appropriate wide-mouthed headset wrench (or a large crescent if home, or channel locks on the road), loosen the large locknut at the top of the headset. Next, loosen the top threaded race, but only slightly, until you can see the bearings but *before* they can escape (something that won't happen if you have the ball-retainer rings common to many bikes today; they also won't fall out as easily—and yet are a bit more difficult to see—if your headset has the rubber or plastic "shields" against water entry).

Now, if I'm in a hurry, and especially if I've been on the road in winter for more than a month and am still not home, I do a quick-lube service of lifting the bars sufficiently (after loosening the top threaded race) to a point where I can see the bearings and shoot grease inside. Then I carefully allow the fork to slip down a fraction of an inch to expose the bottom bearings and add grease there. This done, I tighten the top threaded race, then the locknut on top, until there is no upward or downward movement within the headset, but free movement of the fork side to side. One wrench is required to hold the top threaded race from turning as you tighten the locknut with a second wrench.

It is of course far better to do a complete overhaul, taking everything apart and wiping races and bearings clean and then regreasing (much

Bearings in retainer on headset.

Bearings in bottom race.

as you did on the wheels). Be very careful not to get anything out of order when rebuilding, and do not invert the ball retainer; do so and you will feel the problem when turning the handlebars. If the steerer tube (fork tube) is not painted, coat it lightly with grease to counteract the water that may make its way inside. Grease the handlebar stem as well (down the sides and under the head of the expander bolt), and also the wedge threads; steel wedges often develop a great deal of rust.

Brad and Ken told me that most factory bearings are of far better quality than the inexpensive replacements available at most shops. Therefore, clean and replace all good bearings but do not hesitate to toss those that are flaking, pitted, or cracked. The fellows also suggested that when it comes to rebuilding you should straddle the bike, holding the two wrenches before you on the headset (one on the adjustable cup/top threaded race, the other on the locknut). From this position you can hold the former still (once having attained the best of both worlds—free movement side to side, yet no slipping when the bars are lifted and no knocking when the bike is pushed forward and the brakes are applied) while tightening the latter. Make *sure* it's tight, and check your headset a few times in the weeks following maintenance to determine if it has loosened up.

8

PEDALS

BEARING MAINTENANCE

Tools required:

ALLEN WRENCHES (for some, to remove outer pedal-guard)

SCREWDRIVER

SOCKET WRENCH AND SOCKET (or thin-jawed channel locks)

NEEDLE-NOSE PLIERS (sometimes)

Once again, so-called sealed pedals are, ninety-nine percent of the time, only shielded. And because we're also once again dealing with a part of the bike that can go for years without acting up, pedals are neglected. Chances are, therefore, that when you finally do get around to trying to locate that annoying click when you're pedaling, you'll find very dry, very brown bearings.

Begin by removing the oval outer pedal-guard (not present on all models) with a very small allen wrench. A larger allen is then needed to remove the pedal spindle (axle) cap; on most there is simply a plastic dustcap that takes its place. (Some in-shop knowledge: If the dustcap sits flush with the pedal body, it pries off; if it sits above, it screws off. Usually.) This is as far as some people ever get with pedals, and that's farther than most. They unscrew or pry up the cap, look in at the locknut, lockwasher, cone, and bearings, squirt some grease inside, and

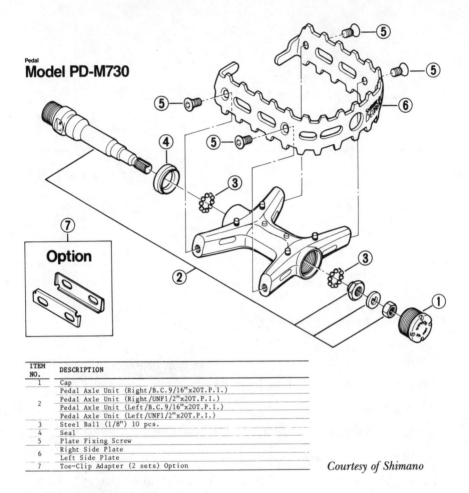

Pedal
Model PD-M730

ITEM NO.	DESCRIPTION
1	Cap
2	Pedal Axle Unit (Right/B.C.9/16"x20T.P.I.)
	Pedal Axle Unit (Right/UNF1/2"x20T.P.I.)
	Pedal Axle Unit (Left/B.C.9/16"x20T.P.I.)
	Pedal Axle Unit (Left/UNF1/2"x20T.P.I.)
3	Steel Ball (1/8") 10 pcs.
4	Seal
5	Plate Fixing Screw
6	Right Side Plate
	Left Side Plate
7	Toe-Clip Adapter (2 sets) Option

Courtesy of Shimano

replace the cap. Presto.

What they don't seem to know, or care about, is that pedals have bearings on *both* sides of the pedal axle. So, if this kind of quick and dirty maintenance appeals to you, at least pry off the back dustcap as well (the side closer to the crankarm) and give those bearings a drink. They'll appreciate it.

But if you really wish to make your pedals happy, try removing first the locknut (easiest with a socket wrench, due to the pedal housing), then the lockwasher, and then the cone. Some pedals have cones with serrated faces, to make unscrewing them an easy task with a screwdriver tip. Others require a needle-nose pliers, or anything else (plus patience) that will reach that deeply into your pedal housing. Once free, the pedal body will slide off, granting access to the rear bearings.

Model : PL-5100

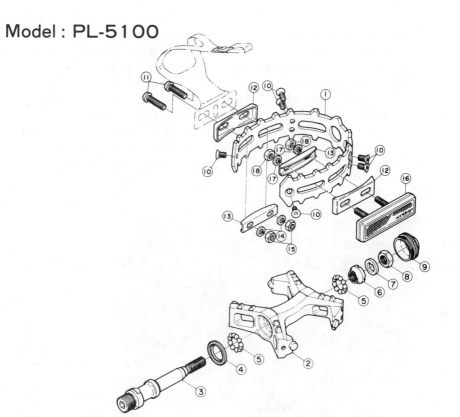

Refer No.	Code No.
1	53250420
2	
3	53250201
3	53250211
4	53251901
5	50138735
6	53321501
7	53328001
8	53325211
9	53250601
10	53293205
11	55205444

Refer No.	Code No.
12	53251001
13	53250801
14	28232400
15	20005571
16	53251201
17	53258401
18	53255501

This will be a snap if you've already worked on your wheel hubs. (It also seems easier to me if I leave the pedals attached to the bike crank-arms when I'm pulling maintenance.) Clean and inspect as before, then rebuild using a great deal of grease (any extra will just work its way out). Snug the cone against the bearings as with all bearings on a bike: enough to prevent sideplay but still allow free rotation. Replace the lockwasher, then use the locknut to hold everything in place. As before, expect to have to loosen the locknut and readjust the cone once or twice before attaining the best of both worlds.

Pedal dust cap removed, exposing locknut.

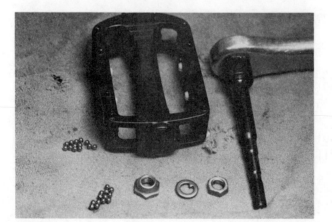

Pedal disassembled.

9

CHAINRINGS AND BOTTOM BRACKETS

Once more, my quarter-century of serious cycling (that is, since my first long tour) is an advantage. This is because I recall the horrible days when it was necessary to extract cotter pins from crankarms (for the pins held the arms in place) before one could begin overhauling a bottom bracket. Driving the pins out with a few licks from a ball peen was usually impossible, for the things most often were frozen in place. Next I would try drilling out the pins, in hopes they would collapse on themselves when whacked a few dozen more times. Then came the propane torch applied to the crankarms to make them expand away from the cotters. Finally, if still unable to extract them, I would hang my head in failure and push the bike to the shop.

And all that just to *reach* the bottom bracket. No wonder, then, that pulling crankarms today—a wonderfully simple accomplishment made possible by unscrewing a couple of bolts—and then greasing my "BB" bearings seems a very light chore. But to the post-cotter-pin generation this comparatively painless task must nevertheless seem extremely troublesome. Why else would so many people today never work on this part of their bikes?

The following paragraphs are designed to step you easily through this procedure. It is not difficult and can in fact be shortened greatly by my own very lazy method of working entirely from the left side of the bike (by reaching through the bracket for the right-side bearings), thereby not removing the chainrings and fixed cup at all. You will in time have to replace a worn-out chainring, however, or may wish to

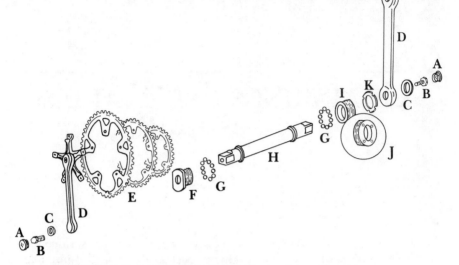

Crank assembly. A) dust cap B) fixing bolt C) washer D) crankarm E) chainrings/chainwheels F) fixed cup G) bearings H) spindle I) adjustable cap J) front view of adjustable cap K) lockring

alter your gearing by substituting another chainring, or may indeed find that working from both sides of the bike allows a more thorough and precise repair. Whichever you decide, the following will tell you how to accomplish it.

Oh yes—one more thing before we begin. Don't become confused by the double names for many of the pieces involved—crankarms/cranks, chainrings/chainwheels, axle/spindle/crankshaft—or by the selective use of some terms. "Sprocket," for example, is used to refer either to chainrings or individual cogs on the freewheel "cluster" (a word meaning the group of five, six, or seven sprockets on the rear wheel). Yet while "cog," according to *Webster's,* can be used for any notched wheel (each notch is also called a "tooth"), in biking it refers almost exclusively to cluster sprockets—not the chainrings. Got it?

CHAINRING REMOVAL/DISASSEMBLY

Tools required:

SMALL ALLEN WRENCH OR CONE WRENCH (to remove dustcaps)

ALLEN WRENCH (for chainring removal)

Close-up of crankarm and chainwheel.

COTTERLESS-CRANK REMOVAL TOOL (or universal crank wrench and crankarm puller)

Begin by removing the two metal or plastic crankarm dustcaps. Some are fitted for an allen; most have a slot that can be reached with a quarter, wide-bladed screwdriver (or smaller one held at an angle), or, in a manner preferred by Ken and Brad, the side of a cone wrench. I've been frustrated in the past by having metal caps freeze up on me during winter rides or rust any time of year, and thus I give mine a toss the first time I pull maintenance. But our mechanics suggest reinstallation; the caps keep crank threads clean, which makes it easy to screw in the crank-removal tool.

Once these are out you can see the crankarm-fixing bolts. Universal tools have heads fitted for various sizes of bolts; crank tools made specifically for one type of crank will have one end that fits the crankarm

Close-up of crankarm fixing bolt.

Universal tool on crankarm fixing bolt.

bolt and the other end beveled to accept the jaws of a large crescent or a short breaker-bar assembly to twist off the bolt. (Except for the Sugino "Autex" crankarm bolt-puller system, that is. As mentioned in the first chapter, the Autex employs a special heavy-duty dustcap that acts as a puller when a six-millimeter allen wrench is applied.)

But back to the more usual crank pullers. Remove the crankarm bolt (let's assume we're working with the right-chainring side) or, in the case of "nutted assemblies" found on many bikes, the nut, and *don't* forget to remove the washer as well. Fail to pull out the washer and the next step will not work. (Crankarm bolts or nuts on both sides are removed counterclockwise.)

Universal crank removal tool in place.

With your fingers alone (so as not to strip threads), start the crank-arm puller into the crankarm, then use a wrench to screw it in as far as it will go. Be sure the threads mesh perfectly.

Now insert the extractor portion—that piece that turns through the inside of the puller—into the puller body; turn it by hand until you feel its tip engage the spindle (axle) end. With a breaker bar, large crescent, or universal tool, turn the extractor clockwise; you will see the chainring assembly begin to slide toward you, away from and off the spindle. Lift the chain off the chainring, place it out of the way on the bottom bracket housing, and remove the left-side crankarm in the same manner.

This is an excellent time to clean your chainrings and to make sure the "chainring fixing bolts"—those that hold the sprockets together, located near the "spider" (the five metal arms radiating out from the crankarm to the attachment points for the chainrings)—are tight. By the way, it is a good idea every now and then to check that these are tight. They seldom come loose, but if they do they'll produce an untrue chainring and cause chain rub and noise on the front derailleur cage. The individual chainrings can be separated easily by using an allen wrench to remove these fixing bolts, and then lifting off the rings. This will be done if you are replacing a worn sprocket or altering your gear pattern. Again, be careful to dismantle and reassemble in exact order; most chainwheels have small spacer washers that must be replaced.

BOTTOM-BRACKET DISASSEMBLY

Tools required:

KNIFE OR SHARP SCREWDRIVER (if bottom bracket is "sealed")

UNIVERSAL ADJUSTABLE-CUP TOOL—also called pin tool (or hammer and punch)

LOCKRING/FIXED-CUP BOTTOM-BRACKET TOOL

Once the crankarms are removed, you can proceed to the bottom bracket. As I mentioned, I remove only the adjustable (left-side) cup when pulling maintenance, thereby making chainring removal unnecessary. You will find the fixed cup to be difficult, because it usually is nearly frozen in place and has a very thin "face" to grip with a wrench.

Fixed cup bottom bracket tool.

(It must be thin to fit between the chainrings and bottom bracket.) The lockring/fixed-cup tool is a must. Back out the cup. (Almost all ATBs are "English threaded," so when looking at the cup you will turn it clockwise for removal.)

Moving to the adjustable cup, you will see a notched lockring surrounding it. The lockring/fixed-cup tool is best for its removal, though on the road, when desperate, I've used screwdrivers and the flat side of a crescent. In time, however, the lockring is ruined this way; besides, you shouldn't need to mess with your bottom bracket on the road unless you've been out for a year or so, or under water for a week. Using the proper tool, engage the angled tip in a lockring notch and remove it—counterclockwise. Now use an adjustable cut tool to engage the "pin holes" (or slots) in the cup's face, and back it out completely.

Nutted-assembly-type bottom bracket (rather than bolt type).

If your bottom bracket is sealed, remove the seal as described in the wheel-bearing-maintenance discussion earlier, by slipping a knife blade or thin screwdriver tip beneath it and prying upward. Many nonsealed systems will have a removable plastic sheath inside, designed to shed some of the water that leaks into the frame if all frame holes have not been plugged (something that should be done immediately upon purchasing a bike), and which pours into the frame if, to prevent theft, you take your saddle and seatpost with you when leaving your bike. Many people do this, especially on campuses, apparently failing to consider the internal (frame tubing and bottom bracket) consequences. Use a Hite Rite, Seat Leash, or thin cable and lock to secure your post and saddle *and* protect your frame innards.

The ball bearings will probably be in a retainer ring. If so, notice in which direction the retainer faces as you remove the spindle; the solid back of the retainer should face *away* from you. Also notice if one end of the spindle is longer than the other. Many axles today are symmetrical, but if one side is longer it will extend toward the chainrings. Clean, inspect, and if necessary replace bearings. Wipe all surfaces clean and inspect the spindle and cups for bearing wear.

Adjustable cup tool.

Adjustable cup removed, exposing plastic sleeve.

*Bearings
repacked.*

BOTTOM-BRACKET REASSEMBLY

Tools required:

THOSE LISTED ABOVE FOR DISASSEMBLY

After thorough cleaning and close inspection, apply a generous bead of grease on the inside of your fixed cup, replace the bearings, and cover them with a second layer of grease. Thread this cup back into the frame (right side, chainring side) with your fingers first, then by using

Adjustable cup tool and adjustable cup lockring tool.

"What's wrong with this picture?"

the tool, snugging it well. To insure easy removal months in the future, apply a bit of grease to the threads inside the bottom bracket before replacing cups. (Note that if you have not removed this fixed cup you will have to reach through the bottom bracket, and from the right side through the spindle hole, to clean/lube/replace bearings.)

Lubricate and replace the bearings in the adjustable cup in the same manner, but do not yet thread the cup into place.

Take the cleaned spindle, longer side (if there is one) toward the fixed cup and, after slipping it through the plastic sleeve, carefully guide it through the bracket and fixed cup from the left side of the bike.

While holding the spindle by one end, pick up the adjustable cup, engage the spindle in the cup hole, and thread it into the frame a few turns. Move to the right side of the bike for a moment and replace the right-hand crankarm securely. (Do grease the bolt threads—or nut threads if you are working with a nutted assembly. Do *not* grease the crankarm hole, the portion that slides over the spindle.) Now, back on the left side, turn the adjustable cup into the frame until it is finger-tight against the bearings. Screw the lockring onto the adjustable cup and snug it down with the lockring tool. Reach through the frame to grasp the right crankarm and, moving it back and forth, check for side-play. (Hold the crankarm itself when doing this, not the pedal. There is too much play within most pedals for you to get a true feel for bottom-bracket side-play.) If it is too loose, as it probably will be, back off the lockring a bit, tighten the adjustable cup slightly, then retighten the lockring. Remember the technique you learned in other bearing work throughout the bike: You are looking for the best possible combination of no side-play and free spindle rotation.

When the adjustment seems correct, replace the left-side crankarm and check again for your adjustment. Place the arms at both the 6/12 o'clock and 3/9 o'clock positions when doing this. Have patience.

Reinstall the dustcaps and restore the chain to the chainring. Check the tightness of these fixing bolts once a week for the next month.

10

AIRLINE TRAVEL

For many people, mountain biking, much like skiing, is becoming a destination sport. Those who cannot take the time to drive, or ride a train, or put up with the rigors of a bus, must therefore prepare their bikes for air shipment.

Many companies now offer hard- and soft-shelled bike cases, but due to the expense of these items I suspect most people will continue to obtain the throwaway cardboard boxes in which dismantled bikes arrive at the shops. This of course demands that you be able to take your bike apart in such a manner that it will fit inside, and upon arrival be capable of rebuilding the bike properly. (Ken and Brad suggest you call your neighborhood shop several weeks before your departure to insure a box for your frame size.)

BIKE DISMANTLING

Tools required:

6-MM ALLEN WRENCH

PEDAL WRENCH OR VERY THIN CRESCENT, though sometimes an allen will suffice here as well

A glance at the photograph will indicate what must be done: handlebars, pedals, and saddle/seatpost removed, and (with some boxes) the front wheel quick-release skewer as well.

Refer to Chapter 7 for handlebar removal. You will recall that bars are pulled easily, sometimes with simply the turning of the (usually allen-headed) extender-bolt stem, more often with a whack from a mallet or other blunt object to free the wedge nut. Be sure you have released the front brake before doing this, however; consult Chapter 4, or simply squeeze your brake pads together by hand and lift the transverse cable free from the cable carrier (this allows the bars to be lifted away and also facilitates wheel removal).

Shift your rear derailleur into its most inboard position (lowest gear, largest sprocket) to distance it from the side of the box, then remove the handlebars and tape or bungie them to your top tube. If you are concerned about scratches in the paint, wrap the top tube with a t-shirt or some other protection, and tape this in place. Next, flip the front wheel quick-release skewer and remove the wheel. (You might need to remove the q-r skewer from the front wheel. If tight space requires this, be sure to put it in a bag or tape it to the bike so that it will not roll out of the box if a small hole appears.) When this is done, resecure the

Handlebars bungied to top tube.

Pedal wrench removing pedal from crankarm.

transverse cable to both brake arms to pull the pads back together and away from the sides of the box.

Remove both pedals, either with a pedal wrench or a crescent thin enough to fit between the crankarm and pedal body. A third (and more difficult) method is to use a beefy allen wrench from the back side, if your pedal is fitted for one. As with the q-r wheel skewer, place the pedals inside a box or bag, attach them with tape or a bungie to the frame, or reattach them to the crankarms—toward the frame.

Remove the saddle and seatpost, plug the hole with a cork or cloth, and gently place the bike into the box in the same manner you see in the photograph. (Racers place a plastic, foam, or cardboard box between their fork blades for protection; most mountain bikers do not.) Don't worry about letting the air out of tires; most luggage compartments are pressurized, and even if they were not, the difference in air

Breakdown of bike enabling it to fit inside the box shown.

pressure between ground level and, say, thirty-five thousand feet is not sufficient to blow most tires. Most tires today are rated far below what they and any good rims can hold.

Finally, pad the bike with clothing and sleeping bags. And *don't* forget the tools required on the other end to put your bike back together.

APPENDICES

APPENDIX A: *Gear Chart for 26" Wheel*

Number of teeth in front sprocket

	24	26	28	30	32	34	36	38	40	42	44	46	48	50	52
12	52	56.3	60.7	65	69.3	73.4	78	82.3	86.7	91	95.3	99.7	104	108.3	112.7
13	48	52	56	60	64	68	72	76	80	84	88	92	96	100	104
14	44.6	48.3	52	55.8	59.4	63.1	66.9	70.6	74.3	78	81.7	85.4	89.1	92.9	96.6
15	41.6	45.1	48.5	52	55.5	58.9	62.4	65.9	69.3	72.8	76.3	79.7	83.2	86.7	90.1
16	39	42.3	45.5	48.8	52	55.3	58.5	61.8	65	68.3	71.5	74.8	78	81.3	84.5
17	36.7	39.8	42.8	45.9	48.9	52	55.1	58.1	61.2	64.2	67.3	70.4	73.4	76.5	79.5
18	34.7	37.6	40.4	43.3	46.2	49.1	52	54.9	57.8	60.7	63.6	66.4	69.3	72.2	75.1
19	32.8	35.6	38.3	41.1	43.8	46.5	49.3	52	54.7	57.8	60.2	62.9	65.7	68.4	71.2
20	31.2	33.8	36.4	39	41.6	44.2	46.8	49.4	52	54.6	57.2	59.8	62.4	65	67.6
21	29.7	32.2	34.7	37.1	39.6	42.1	44.6	47	49.5	52	54.5	57	59.4	61.9	63.4
22	28.4	30.7	33.1	35.5	37.8	40.2	42.5	44.9	47.3	49.6	52	54.4	56.7	59.1	61.5
23	27.1	29.4	31.7	33.9	36.2	38.4	40.7	43	45.2	47.5	49.7	52	54.3	56.5	58.8
24	26	28.2	30.3	32.5	34.7	36.8	39	41.2	43.3	45.5	47.7	49.8	52	54.2	56.3
25	25	27	29.1	31.2	33.3	35.4	37.4	39.5	41.6	43.7	45.8	47.8	49.9	52	54.1
26	24	26	28	30	32	34	36	38	40	42	44	46	48	50	52
27	23.1	25	27	28.9	30.8	32.7	34.7	36.6	38.5	40.4	42.4	44.3	46.2	48.1	50.1
28	22.3	24.1	26	27.9	29.7	31.6	33.4	35.3	37.1	39	40.9	42.7	44.6	46.4	48.3
29	21.5	23.3	25.1	26.9	28.7	30.5	32.3	34.1	35.9	37.7	39.4	41.2	43	44.8	46.6
30	20.8	22.5	24.3	26	27.7	29.5	31.2	32.9	34.7	36.4	38.1	39.9	41.6	43.3	45.1
31	20.1	21.8	23.5	25.2	26.8	28.5	30.2	31.9	33.5	35.2	36.9	38.6	40.3	41.9	43.6
32	19.5	21.1	22.8	24.4	26	27.6	29.3	30.9	32.5	34.1	35.8	37.4	39	40.6	42.3
33	18.9	20.5	22.1	23.6	25.2	26.7	28.4	29.9	31.5	33.1	34.7	36.2	37.8	39.4	41
34	18.4	19.9	21.4	22.9	24.5	26	27.5	29.1	30.6	32.1	33.6	35.2	36.7	38.2	39.8
35	17.8	19.3	20.8	22.3	23.8	25.3	26.7	28.2	29.7	31.2	32.7	34.2	35.7	37.1	38.6
36	17.3	18.8	20.2	21.7	23.1	24.6	26	27.4	28.9	30.3	31.8	33.2	34.7	36.1	37.6

Number of teeth in rear sprocket

$$\text{inch gear} \ = \ \frac{\text{\# teeth in front sprocket}}{\text{\# teeth in rear sprocket}} \ \times \ \text{wheel diameter in inches}$$

Example: $\frac{48}{13} \ \times \ 26 \ = \ 96$ inch gear

(Compute linear distance traveled with each crank rotation by multiplying "inch gear" by pi = 3.14)

Example: $96 \ \times \ 3.14 \ = \ 301.44''$ (or $25.12'$ linear distance)

APPENDIX B: *Maintenance Schedule*

Author's Note

I wish to make it clear that the following is our *mechanics'* suggested maintenance schedule—not mine. Like most mountain bikers who commute daily, year-round (in addition to normal trail and dirt-road riding), I inflate my tires once a week, pay attention to any noises coming from my drive train (usually indicating a dry chain or derailleur out of adjustment), and attempt to notice the slightest of differences in the overall *feel* of the bike while I'm pedaling. I explained this to Ken and Brad. They smiled wanly, shook their heads, then returned to working on a bike whose owner follows *my* usual maintenance pattern.

This schedule is based upon an average riding frequency of two to three times per week, with an "average ride" being two to four hours long. Less riding extends the time between one-month, three-month, and annual maintenance. Occasional riders (three or four times per month) can often go two years between complete overhauls. Frequent and high-mileage riders (more than two or three thousand miles annually) might need to overhaul the bike twice a year—depending upon riding style (gentle, slightly abusive, criminal) and environment (dust, rain, snow, mud, lava, quicksand . . .). Regardless of the rider we (the mechanics, remember) recommend an overhaul on a new bike during the first year—to replace the factory grease with that of higher quality and greater quantity.

Before Each Ride

1. Make any needed repairs and replace missing items in repair kit.

2. Wheels:
   Make sure they are securely attached to the bike.
   Wiggle them side to side to check for loose cones.
   Spin slowly to check for too-tight cones.
   Inspect rims for nicks and damage to braking surface.
   Inspect for true while rotating rims.
   Inspect tires for cuts and foreign objects.
   Are tires inflated properly for existing conditions?

3. Brakes:
   Are all cables hooked up properly?

Pull brake levers; does brake action feel normal?

Make sure pads are striking rim properly.

4. Headset:

    With front brake applied, rock bike forward and backward to check for loose headset.

    Lift front of bike off ground and turn handlebars to check for rough spin or too-tight rotation.

5. Wiggle crankarms to check for loose bottom bracket.

    Spin crank backwards to check for tight bottom bracket. (You may have to remove chain from chainrings to prevent jamming.)

6. Wiggle pedals to check for loose adjustment.

    Spin pedals to check for tight adjustment.

7. Drive train:

    Inspect derailleurs for damage or misalignment.

    Is chain sufficiently lubed?

8. Check saddle height and quick-release skewer for proper adjustment.

9. Before riding away, lift rear wheel off ground and slowly pedal bike to make sure chain is not between gears, and that drive train sounds okay.

10. Additional steps if bike has been subjected to excessive sand, mud, water:

    Wipe dirt and mud from brakes, derailleurs and chain.

    Lube shift cable guides at bottom bracket.

    Lube derailleur pivot points.

    Lube chain.

    Wipe braking surface on rims.

    Call a cab, 'cause if you've done all the above you're going to need one to get to work or school on time. (My words.)

Monthly

[In addition to the steps in "Before Each Ride"]

Inspect chain, chainrings, freewheel and rear derailleur pulleys for build-up of dirt and grease.

If needed, remove chain and clean in solvent.

Wipe chainrings, freewheel and pulleys with rag and solvent.

If rear derailleur pulleys do not spin smoothly, remove and lube bushings.

Every Three Months

In addition to the steps in "Before Each Ride" and "Every Three Months"

1. Inspect tires for wear. If needed switch tires between front and rear to extend life.

2. Inspect rims for rubber build-up on brake surfaces. Clean with solvent and coarse rag or steel wool. Rough up brake pads with emery cloth and wipe with clean dry rag. Inspect rims for dents, nicks, and bulges around spoke nipples. Inspect spokes for proper tension (that is, roughly the same tension on all).

3. Pull brakes off pivots and check status of grease on pivots. If needed wipe clean and apply fresh grease.

4. With brake cable disengaged, check action of levers and cables. If needed, pull cables and lube.

5. Check shift cables; pull and lube if necessary.

Annually

In addition to all steps above.

1. Disassembly and overhaul of bike (headset, hubs, bottom bracket, pedals).

2. Grease stem and seatpost.

3. Check chain, chainrings, freewheel, derailleur pulleys, brake pad for wear. Flush freewheel in solvent and re-lube.

4. True wheels on a wheel jig if needed.

5. If it moves, lube it.

APPENDIX C: *Instruction Sheets/Exploded Drawings*

Shimano Total Integration (STI) System

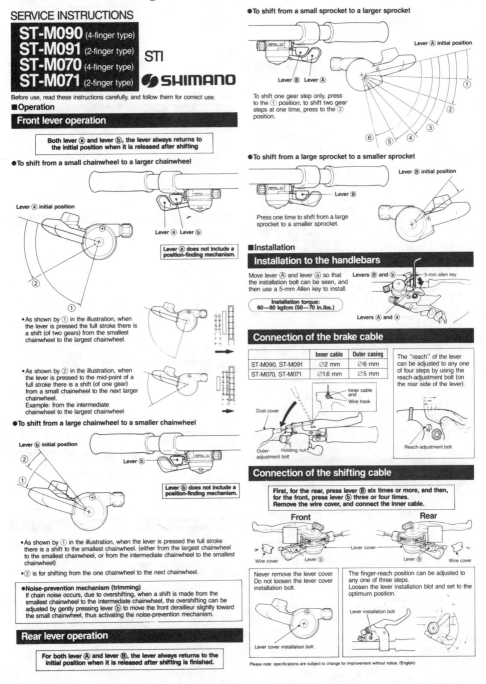

SERVICE INSTRUCTIONS

ST-M090 (4-finger type)
ST-M091 (2-finger type) **STI**
ST-M070 (4-finger type)
ST-M071 (2-finger type) **SHIMANO**

Before use, read these instructions carefully, and follow them for correct use.

■Operation

Front lever operation

Both lever ⓐ and lever ⓑ, the lever always returns to the initial position when it is released after shifting

●To shift from a small chainwheel to a larger chainwheel

Lever ⓐ initial position

Lever ⓐ Lever ⓑ

Lever ⓐ does not include a position-finding mechanism.

• As shown by ① in the illustration, when the lever is pressed the full stroke there is a shift (of two gears) from the smallest chainwheel to the largest chainwheel.

• As shown by ② in the illustration, when the lever is pressed to the mid-point of a full stroke there is a shift (of one gear) from a small chainwheel to the next larger chainwheel.
Example: from the intermediate chainwheel to the largest chainwheel

●To shift from a large chainwheel to a smaller chainwheel

Lever ⓑ initial position

Lever ⓑ

Lever ⓑ does not include a position-finding mechanism.

• As shown by ① in the illustration, when the lever is pressed the full stroke there is a shift to the smallest chainwheel. (either from the largest chainwheel to the smallest chainwheel, or from the intermediate chainwheel to the smallest chainwheel)

•② is for shifting from the one chainwheel to the next chainwheel.

●Noise-prevention mechanism (trimming)
If chain noise occurs, due to overshifting, when a shift is made from the smallest chainwheel to the intermediate chainwheel, the overshifting can be adjusted by gently pressing lever ⓑ to move the front derailleur slightly toward the small chainwheel, thus activating the noise-prevention mechanism.

Rear lever operation

For both lever Ⓐ and lever Ⓑ, the lever always returns to the initial position when it is released after shifting is finished.

●To shift from a small sprocket to a larger sprocket

Lever Ⓐ initial position

Lever Ⓑ Lever Ⓐ

To shift one gear step only, press to the ① position; to shift two gear steps at one time, press to the ② position.

①
②
③
⑥ ⑤ ④

●To shift from a large sprocket to a smaller sprocket

Lever Ⓑ initial position

Lever Ⓑ

Press one time to shift from a large sprocket to a smaller sprocket.

■Installation

Installation to the handlebars

Move lever Ⓐ and lever ⓐ so that the installation bolt can be seen, and then use a 5-mm Allen key to install.

Levers Ⓑ and ⓑ ——— 5-mm allen key

Installation torque:
60—80 kgfcm (50—70 in.lbs.)

Levers Ⓐ and ⓐ

Connection of the brake cable

	Inner cable	Outer casing
ST-M090, ST-M091	⌀2 mm	⌀6 mm
ST-M070, ST-M071	⌀1.6 mm	⌀5 mm

The "reach" of the lever can be adjusted to any one of four steps by using the reach-adjustment bolt (on the rear side of the lever).

Inner cable end
Wire hook

Dust cover

Outer-adjustment bolt
Holding nut

Reach-adjustment bolt

Connection of the shifting cable

First, for the rear, press lever Ⓑ six times or more, and then, for the front, press lever ⓑ three or four times.
Remove the wire cover, and connect the inner cable.

Front   **Rear**

Wire cover   Lever ⓑ   Lever cover   Lever Ⓑ   Wire cover

Never remove the lever cover. Do not loosen the lever cover installation bolt.

The finger-reach position can be adjusted to any one of three steps. Loosen the lever installation blot and set to the optimum position.

Lever installation bolt

Lever cover installation bolt

Please note: specifications are subject to change for improvement without notice. (English)

SERVICE INSTRUCTIONS

ST-M060
ST-M050-R/L STI

Before use, read these instructions carefully, and follow them for correct use.

■Operation

Rear lever operation

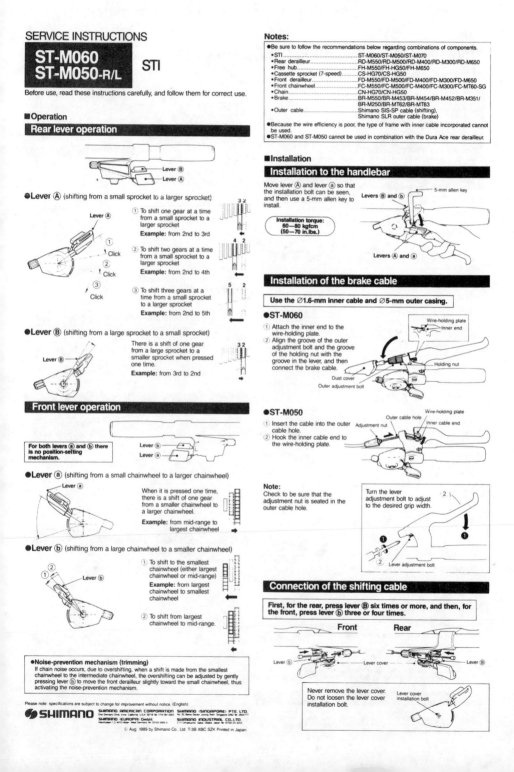

●Lever Ⓐ (shifting from a small sprocket to a larger sprocket)

Lever Ⓐ

① Click
② Click
③ Click

① To shift one gear at a time from a small sprocket to a larger sprocket
Example: from 2nd to 3rd

② To shift two gears at a time from a small sprocket to a larger sprocket
Example: from 2nd to 4th

③ To shift three gears at a time from a small sprocket to a larger sprocket
Example: from 2nd to 5th

●Lever Ⓑ (shifting from a large sprocket to a small sprocket)

Lever Ⓑ

There is a shift of one gear from a large sprocket to a smaller sprocket when pressed one time.
Example: from 3rd to 2nd

Front lever operation

For both levers ⓐ and ⓑ there is no position-setting mechanism.

Lever ⓑ
Lever ⓐ

●Lever ⓐ (shifting from a small chainwheel to a larger chainwheel)

Lever ⓐ

When it is pressed one time, there is a shift of one gear from a smaller chainwheel to a larger chainwheel.
Example: from mid-range to largest chainwheel

●Lever ⓑ (shifting from a large chainwheel to a smaller chainwheel)

② ① Lever ⓑ

① To shift to the smallest chainwheel (either largest chainwheel or mid-range)
Example: from largest chainwheel to smallest chainwheel

② To shift from largest chainwheel to mid-range.

●Noise-prevention mechanism (trimming)
If chain noise occurs, due to overshifting, when a shift is made from the smallest chainwheel to the intermediate chainwheel, the overshifting can be adjusted by gently pressing lever ⓑ to move the front derailleur slightly toward the small chainwheel, thus activating the noise-prevention mechanism.

Please note: specifications are subject to change for improvement without notice. (English)

Ⓢ SHIMANO SHIMANO AMERICAN CORPORATION SHIMANO (SINGAPORE) PTE. LTD.
SHIMANO (EUROPA) GmbH SHIMANO INDUSTRIAL CO., LTD.
© Aug. 1989 by Shimano Co., Ltd. T-3B XBC SZK Printed in Japan.

Notes:

●Be sure to follow the recommendations below regarding combinations of components.
- STI...ST-M060/ST-M050/ST-M070
- Rear derailleur.........................RD-M550/RD-M500/RD-M400/RD-M300/RD-M650
- Free hub....................................FH-M550/FH-HG50/FH-M650
- Cassette sprocket (7-speed)..........CS-HG70/CS-HG50
- Front derailleur.......................FD-M550/FD-M500/FD-M400/FD-M300/FD-M650
- Front chainwheel.....................FC-M550/FC-M500/FC-M400/FC-M300/FC-MT60-SG
- Chain..CN-HG70/CN-HG50
- Brake.......................................BR-M550/BR-M453/BR-M454/BR-M452/BR-M351/ BR-M250/BR-MT62/BR-MT63
- Outer cable............................Shimano SIS-SP cable (shifting), Shimano SLR outer cable (brake)

●Because the wire efficiency is poor, the type of frame with inner cable incorporated cannot be used.
●ST-M060 and ST-M050 cannot be used in combination with the Dura Ace rear derailleur.

■Installation

Installation to the handlebar

Move lever Ⓐ and lever ⓐ so that the installation bolt can be seen, and then use a 5-mm allen key to install.

5-mm allen key
Levers Ⓑ and ⓑ

Installation torque:
60—80 kgfcm
(50—70 in.lbs.)

Levers Ⓐ and ⓐ

Installation of the brake cable

Use the ∅1.6-mm inner cable and ∅5-mm outer casing.

●ST-M060

① Attach the inner end to the wire-holding plate.
② Align the groove of the outer adjustment bolt and the groove of the holding nut with the groove in the lever, and then connect the brake cable.

Wire-holding plate
Inner end
Holding nut
Dust cover
Outer adjustment bolt

●ST-M050

① Insert the cable into the outer cable hole.
② Hook the inner cable end to the wire-holding plate.

Wire-holding plate
Adjustment nut
Outer cable hole
Inner cable end

Note:
Check to be sure that the adjustment nut is seated in the outer cable hole.

Turn the lever adjustment bolt to adjust to the desired grip width.

Lever adjustment bolt

Connection of the shifting cable

First, for the rear, press lever Ⓑ six times or more, and then, for the front, press lever ⓑ three or four times.

Front   Rear

Lever ⓑ   Lever cover   Lever Ⓑ

Never remove the lever cover. Do not loosen the lever cover installation bolt.

Lever cover installation bolt

Notes when securing the inner cable

●Rear

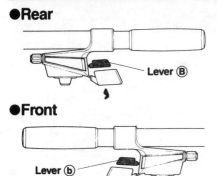

Lever ⑧

After pressing the STI lever ⑧ **six times or more** (so that the lever is set for the smallest sprocket), connect the inner cable.

●Front

Lever ⓑ

After pressing the STI lever ⓑ **three or four times** (so that the lever is set for the smallest chainwheel), connect the inner cable.

STI cable tension adjustment (front derailleur)

① Set the chain to the **largest rear sprocket,** and, at the front, use the STI to shift **from the largest chainwheel to the intermediate chainwheel.**

Largest sprocket   Largest chainwheel

Largest sprocket   Intermediate chainwheel

② Adjust, by using the STI's outer-adjustment bolt, so that there is the minimum clearance, but so that the chain and the plate (inside the chain guide) do not contact.

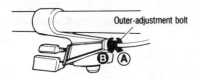

Outer-adjustment bolt

Ⓑ Ⓐ

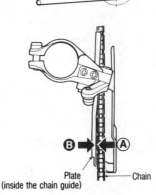

Ⓑ ➡ ◄ Ⓐ

Plate (inside the chain guide)   Chain

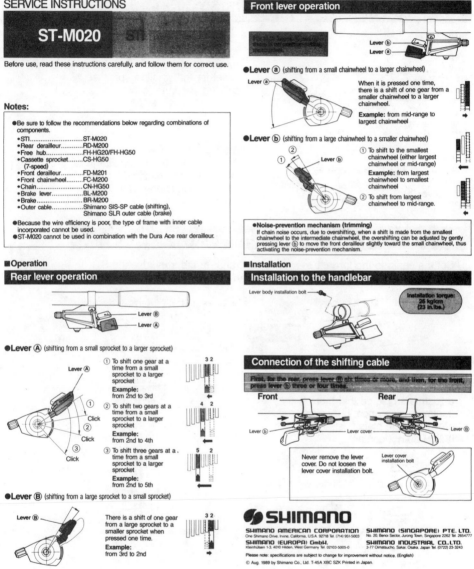

SERVICE INSTRUCTIONS

ST-M020

Before use, read these instructions carefully, and follow them for correct use.

Notes:

- Be sure to follow the recommendations below regarding combinations of components.
  - STI..............................ST-M020
  - Rear derailleur............RD-M200
  - Free hub......................FH-HG20/FH-HG50
  - Cassette sprocket........CS-HG50 (7-speed)
  - Front derailleur.............FD-M201
  - Front chainwheel..........FC-M200
  - Chain..........................CN-HG50
  - Brake lever...................BL-M200
  - Brake..........................BR-M200
  - Outer cable..................Shimano SIS-SP cable (shifting), Shimano SLR outer cable (brake)
- Because the wire efficiency is poor, the type of frame with inner cable incorporated cannot be used.
- ST-M020 cannot be used in combination with the Dura Ace rear derailleur.

■Operation

Rear lever operation

- Lever Ⓐ (shifting from a small sprocket to a larger sprocket)

  ① To shift one gear at a time from a small sprocket to a larger sprocket
  Example: from 2nd to 3rd

  ② To shift two gears at a time from a small sprocket to a larger sprocket
  Example: from 2nd to 4th

  ③ To shift three gears at a time from a small sprocket to a larger sprocket
  Example: from 2nd to 5th

- Lever Ⓑ (shifting from a large sprocket to a small sprocket)

  There is a shift of one gear from a large sprocket to a smaller sprocket when pressed one time.
  Example: from 3rd to 2nd

Front lever operation

- Lever ⓐ (shifting from a small chainwheel to a larger chainwheel)

  When it is pressed one time, there is a shift of one gear from a smaller chainwheel to a larger chainwheel.
  Example: from mid-range to largest chainwheel

- Lever ⓑ (shifting from a large chainwheel to a smaller chainwheel)

  ① To shift to the smallest chainwheel (either largest chainwheel or mid-range)
  Example: from largest chainwheel to smallest chainwheel
  ② To shift from largest chainwheel to mid-range.

- **Noise-prevention mechanism (trimming)**
  If chain noise occurs, due to overshifting, when a shift is made from the smallest chainwheel to the intermediate chainwheel, the overshifting can be adjusted by gently pressing lever ⓑ to move the front derailleur slightly toward the small chainwheel, thus activating the noise-prevention mechanism.

■Installation

Installation to the handlebar

Lever body installation bolt

Installation torque: 26 kgfcm (23 in.lbs.)

Connection of the shifting cable

First, for the rear, press lever Ⓐ six times or more, and then, for the front, press lever ⓑ three or four times.

Front   **Rear**

Lever ⓑ   Lever cover   Lever Ⓑ

Never remove the lever cover. Do not loosen the lever cover installation bolt.

Lever cover installation bolt

🐟 SHIMANO

SHIMANO AMERICAN CORPORATION
One Shimano Drive, Irvine, California, U.S.A. 92718 Tel. (714) 951-5003
SHIMANO (EUROPA) GmbH.
Kleinhülsen 1-3, 4010 Hilden, West Germany Tel. 02103-5005-0

SHIMANO (SINGAPORE) PTE. LTD.
No. 20, Benoi Sector, Jurong Town, Singapore 2262 Tel. 2654777
SHIMANO INDUSTRIAL CO.,LTD.
3-77 Oimatsucho, Sakai, Osaka, Japan Tel. (0722) 23-3243

Please note: specifications are subject to change for improvement without notice. (English)
© Aug. 1989 by Shimano Co., Ltd. T-45A XBC SZK Printed in Japan.

SunTour X-press Control Levers

Model:

SL-PP10-R7U (Code No. 33119571)   SL-PP00-R7U (Code No. 33519571)
7-speed/Right   7-speed/Right
SL-PP10-R6R (Code No. 33119561)   SL-PP00-R6R (Code No. 33519561)
6-speed/Right   6-speed/Right
SL-PP10-L (Code No. 33119701)   SL-PP00-L (Code No.33519701)
Left   Left

To attach this control lever properly, the straight portion of the
handlebars should be: (grip length) + (brake lever bracket length) +
50mm. Please select a handlebar which satisfies this requirement.

1. Attaching to Handlebars
Slide the shift lever along the handlebars. As shown in figure 1,
secure the shift lever at the appropriate position using the
clamp bolt, tightened to a torque of 50 kgf-cm. Figure 1 shows
how to attach the right lever (for the rear derailleur). Follow the
same procedure for the left lever (for the front derailleur).

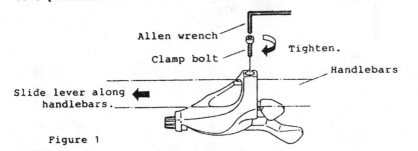

Allen wrench

Clamp bolt   Tighten.

                              Handlebars

Slide lever along
handlebars.

Figure 1

(Note)
If you are not using the X-Press shift levers with Suntour XC Pro or
XCD brake levers, please install the shift levers as shown in figure
1B.
If the angle between the centerlines of the shift and brake levers is
less than 10 degrees, the upshift lever may contact the brake lever
clamp, which may not allow the shift levers to operate properly.

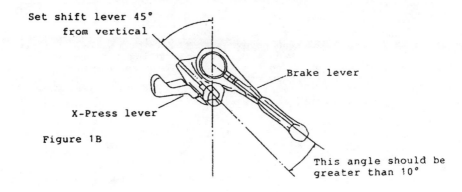

Set shift lever 45°
   from vertical

                              Brake lever

X-Press lever

Figure 1B

                              This angle should be
                              greater than 10°

2. Connecting Inner Cable

Push lever A until lever B returns all the way to its rearmost
position. Loosen the set screw, then slightly turn the shift
lever cover and remove (Fig. 2A).

When connecting the inner cable, keep levers A and B at the
position described above. Insert the inner cable end into the
cable anchor socket and engage the cable. Be aware that the
cable insertion direction for the right lever (rear derailleur)
is opposite that for the left lever (front derailleur). See Figs.
2B and 2C. Pass the inner cable through the outer casing and
stretch the cable until taught.

(NOTE: New X-Press levers are shipped with the cables already
installed. In such cases, simply pass the inner cable through
the outer casing and stretch the cable until taught.)

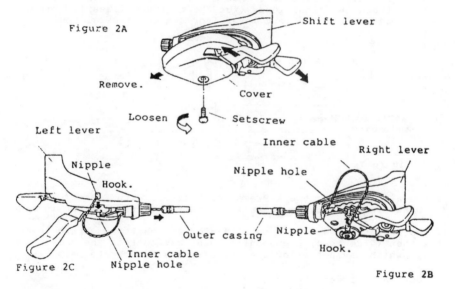

Figure 2A

Shift lever

Remove.

Cover

Loosen   Setscrew

Left lever

Inner cable

Nipple hole

Right lever

Nipple

Outer casing   Nipple

Hook.

Figure 2C   Inner cable
             Nipple hole

Figure 2B

3. Attaching Cover

As shown in figure 3, fit the cover on to the lever handle while **slightly**
turning the cover (in the same way as when removing the cover).
Secure the cover by tightening the setscrew to a torque of 20kgf-cm
(figure 3B). The figures show how to attach the cover to the right
lever (for the rear derailleur). Follow the same procedure for the
left lever (for the front derailleur).

Fit onto lever.

Cover

Setscrew — Tighten.

Figure 3A   Figure 3B

4. Shifting Operation

With the Express Control Lever, you can control shifting simply by pushing levers. The left lever controls INNER-OUTER or OUTER-INNER shifting. When using the left lever, push lever B for INNER-OUTER (figure 4A) and push lever A for OUTER-INNER (figure 4B). When using the right lever, push lever B for TOP-LOW (figure 4C) and push lever A for LOW-TOP (figure 4D). You can quickly shift from TOP to LOW by pushing the lever just once. However, when you want to shift from LOW to TOP, you must shift in incremental steps.

Left Lever   Right Lever

Top-Low

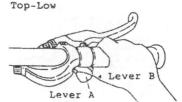

Lever B

Lever A   Inner-Outer

Lever A

Lever B

Figure 4A   Figure 4C

Low-Top

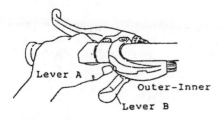

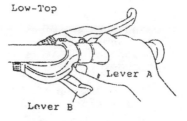

Lever A

Outer-Inner

Lever A

Lever B

Lever B

Figure 4B   Figure 4D

SunTour Accushift Rear Derailleur

C. INSTALLING AND ADJUSTING SUNTOUR ACCUSHIFT REAR DERAILLEURS

1. With a 5mm allen wrench, attach the rear derailleur to the frame so that the derailleur's spring retainer tab is just behind and up against the dropout's derailleur stop (fig. 5). (α-3000 rear derailleurs do not have a spring in the upper pivot, so they will not have this spring retainer tab). Tighten to a torque of 80-100 kgf/cm (fig. 6).

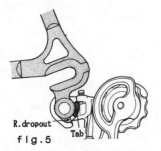

fig.5

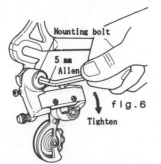

fig.6

2. Adjust the high gear limit screw (H) so that the guide pulley centers <u>directly</u> under the smallest freewheel cog (fig. 7). This adjustment is critical, since the indexing is keyed to this guide pulley position. Clockwise moves the pulley in; counterclockwise moves it out.

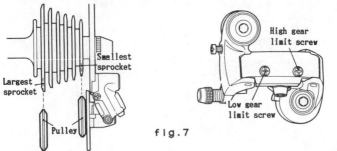

fig.7

3. If using SunTour Index Power Control (IPC) shift levers, set the right hand lever to the Power mode (P). If using Index Friction Control (IFC) levers, set the indicator arrow to Friction mode.

4. Push the right hand shift control lever all the way forward.

fig.8

5. Turn the cable adjusting barrel at the rear of the derailleur (fig. 8) all the way in (clockwise).

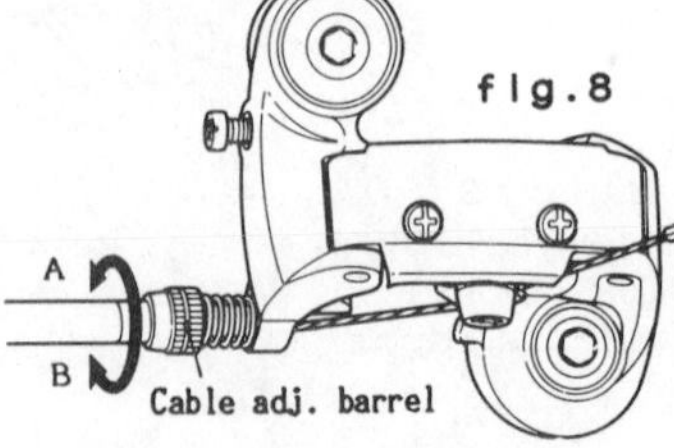

6. Check all cable casing and confirm that it is the correct
type, and the ends are either cleanly squared or capped, or both.
Check shift cable to confirm it is the correct type. (Reference:
"Cables" and "Cable Casing" in Section II B "Strongly Recommended
Components"). Lubricate the inside of all cable casing with a
light oil (grease is **not** acceptable). The lining inside the
casing is not a substitute for lubrication.

7. Loosen the cable anchor bolt. Lead a
new **AccuShift** compatible shifting
control cable from the shift lever through
the cable guides, cable casings, and the
rear derailleur's cable adjusting barrel,
into the cable anchor clamp. Pull the
control cable tight, and tighten the cable
anchor bolt to a torque of 40-50 kgf/cm.
Cut the cable to length and cap it to
prevent fraying (fig. 9).

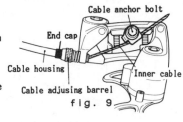

fig. 9

8. Confirm the chain is the correct length by shifting into
highest gear (small freewheel cog & large chainring). Then, while
holding the rear derailleur body **parallel** to the chainstay,
locate the small dot on the pulley cage. (*α*-3000 rear derailleurs
use the cage pivot stop pin as reference instead of a dot.) If
the chain is the correct length, this dot will line up with
specific reference marks on the main body of the rear derailleur.
These are:

Superbe Pro, Sprint-9000: two lines molded into the plastic
bushing between the pulley cage and the main derailleur body
(fig. 10a)

Cyclone-7000, XC-9000, XC Sport-7000, *α*-5000: a small notch in
the alloy of the lower pivot spring housing (fig. 10b)

α-3000: a notch cut into the steel cage hanger tab (fig. 10c)

fig.10a

fig. 10b

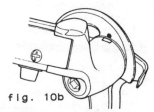

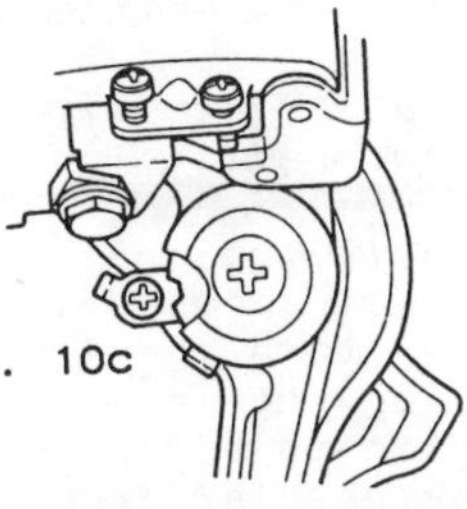

fig. 10c

Add or remove chain lengths as needed.

WARNING: ACCIDENTS CAN RESULT FROM INADEQUATE OR EXCESSIVE CHAIN
LENGTH, OR USING GEARING WHICH EXCEEDS THE REAR DERAILLEUR'S
CAPACITY. <u>ALWAYS</u> use the correct chain length, and gearing within
the rear derailleur's capacity.

9. Shift the rear derailleur into lowest gear (the guide pulley
directly under the largest rear sprocket - fig. 6). If the pulley

will not move far enough, turn the low gear limit screw (L) counterclockwise until it does. Then, turn the (L) adjusting screw clockwise to fine tune the rear derailleur so it shifts the chain consistently onto the largest cog without shifting it between the freewheel and the spokes.

WARNING: Maladjustment of the rear derailleur can cause the chain to shift off the freewheel, leading to possible loss of control of the bike, and injury to the rider.

10. With the rear derailleur still in lowest gear, pull back firmly on the shift lever (<u>don't</u> overdo it!) to stretch the cable and settle the cable casing. Then, push the lever all the way forward; loosen the cable anchor bolt; pull all the slack out of the cable; and retighten the cable anchor bolt to a torque of 40-50 kgf/cm.

11. Shift the chain on to the inner chainring and the largest freewheel sprocket. Using the angle adjusting screw (fig. 11), move the guide pulley up as close to the largest freewheel sprocket as you can. If it is too close, the rear derailleur will not be able to shift the chain off of the largest cog. In this case, move the guide pulley away from the largest cog, again using the angle adjusting screw, until the rear derailleur can shift the chain off the largest cog onto the second cog. If the chain will not shift off the largest cog, even with the derailleur all the way back, the "largest sprocket" capacity of the rear derailleur has been exceeded. Replace it with a rear derailleur that has a longer cage.

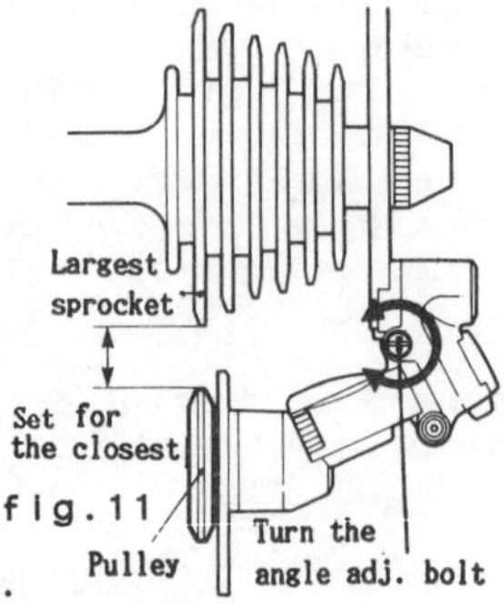

Largest sprocket

Set for the closest

fig.11

Pulley

Turn the angle adj. bolt

12. Turn the cranks forward and shift the shift lever back and forwards several times. If the derailleur overshifts on either the smallest or the largest sprocket, turn the appropriate limit adjusting screw clockwise. If the derailleur undershifts, turn the appropriate limit screw clockwise. **CAUTION**: This adjustment must be precise for safe operation of the bike.

13. Shift the chain onto the outer chainring and smallest freewheel sprocket. Set the levers to index mode. (With IPC levers, turn the indicator dial to "UL" for Ultra-7 freewheels; "RE" for regular spaced freewheels. With IFC levers, loosten the friction adjusting screw no more than 2 full turns, and turn the indicator dial from "friction" to "index". Then, re-tighten the frictin adjusting screw.) Turning the cranks forward, shift the lever one stop. Whenever shifting to a larger cog, remember to hold the lever against the built-in "lash" described under "IFC Levers" in Section II A. The chain may or may not shift onto the second outboard cog. If it doesn't shift, or if it does and the chain grinds, take one of the following steps:

a. If the chain does not move far enough to smoothly engage
the second sprocket (undershift), gradually turn the cable
adjusting barrel (fig. 8) counterclockwise untill you have smooth
shifting.

b. If the chain moves too far (overshift), gradually turn the
cable adjusting barrel (fig. 8) clockwise untill you have smooth
shifting.

14. Fine tuning is accomplished by shifting in rapid succession
from one cog to the next, unscrewing the adjusting barrel
(counter-clockwise) for hesitant <u>downshifts</u> (towards inboard
cogs), and screwing the adjusting barrel in (clockwise) for
hesitant <u>upshifts</u> (towards outboard cogs).

15. If fine tuning is difficult, please refer to the checklist
and trouble-shooting guide.

16. Occasionally lubricate pivot points and bearing surfaces with
light oil.

IF IT DOESN'T WORK:

If you encounter shifting problems on an installed AccuShift
system when in the index mode, first check the efficiency of the
cable transmission. With the chain on any except the innermost
cog, move the shift lever just enough to take up the small
ammount of free movement designed into it. The rear derailleur
<u>must</u> move a corresponding ammount. If it does not, there is too
much drag on the cable, and the source of the drag must be
located and eliminated.

Having made this check, if trouble persists check the following
10 points. For details, refer to the appropriate sections in the
preceeding pages.

NOTE: Some bikes will work acceptably even if they do not
conform to all of the recommended dimensions or component
requirements. If it works, don't fix it.

1. LEVER: If IPC levers are used, confirm that the shifter boss
is correctly oriented on the downtube (see diagram). Then,
confirm that the selector dial is set to "UL" for Ultra-7
freewheels, or "RE" for regular 6 & 5 speed freewheels.

If IFC levers are used, confirm that you are not trying to mix α-
3000 components with NON α-3000 components>

2. CABLE: Confirm that the cable is a quality 1.2mm wound type
(available from SunTour).

SunTour Accushift Thumb Shifter

SUNTOUR ACCUSHIFT THUMB SHIFTER

Model:SL-XD00-CH
Code No.31579901(Right), 31579921(Left)
Model:SL-4050-CH
Code No.31559901(Right), 31559921(Left)

INSTRUCTION MANUAL

SL-XD00-CH   SL-4050-CH

IMPORTANT NOTICE:
All Suntour AccuShift shift levers are factory assembled, and are not user serviceable.

SUNTOUR

1 Install the shift lever onto the handle bar. Decide where it should be located, and then tighten the clamp nut with a torque of 50-60 kgf. cm. (Fig. 1) Figure 1 show the installation procedure of the right XCD-6000 shift lever; the same procedure applies to the XCD-6000 and XCD-4050 right and left levers.

Right lever
(Do not disassemble.)

Handle bar

Clamp nut

(Fig. 1)   Tighten

2 Install the inner cable as shown in fig. 2–A. Be certain that the cable head is well seated into the the recess in the lever. For cable installation of the XCD-4050, see fig. 2B. Before connecting the cable to the front or rear derailleur, be sure the lever is rotated all the way back towards the rider's position. Check that the cable is in its groove on the lever.

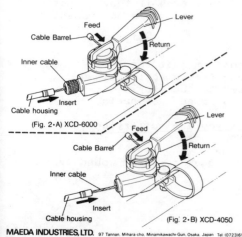

Lever
Feed
Cable Barrel
Return
Inner cable
Insert
Cable housing
(Fig. 2·A) XCD-6000

Lever
Feed
Cable Barrel
Return
Inner cable
Insert
Cable housing   (Fig. 2·B) XCD-4050

3 The XCD-6000 and XCD-4050 right hand shift levers can be selected to shift either in "index" or "friction" mode.

INDEX mode

To switch into the index mode, loosen the friction adjusting bolt counter–clockwise one full turn. Turn the selector ring clockwise until the "index" arrow is aligned with white dot on the pressure disc. Retighten the friction adjusting bolt . (See figures 3–A and 3–B.) (NOTE: the figures show the XCD-6000 lever; the procedure is the same for the XCD-4050 lever.)

Tighten   Loosen (One turn)
Friction adjusting bolt
Turn the selector ring clockwise 60 .
(Fig. 3·A)

Selector ring
Selector ring
Presure disc
In INDEX mode
(Fig. 3·B)

FRICTION mode

To switch to the friction mode, loosen the friction adjusting bolt one full turn. Turn the selector ring counter–clockwise, until the "friction" arrow aligns with the white dot on the pressure disc. Re–tighten the friction adjusting bolt . (See figures 3–C and 3–D.)

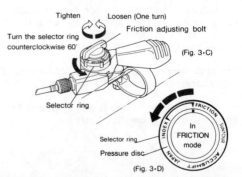

Tighten   Loosen (One turn)
Friction adjusting bolt
Turn the selector ring counterclockwise 60'
(Fig. 3·C)

Selector ring
Selector ring
Pressure disc
In FRICTION mode
(Fig. 3·D)

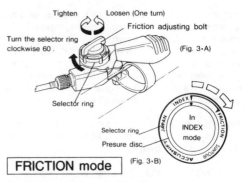
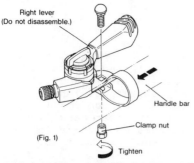

MAEDA INDUSTRIES, LTD. 97 Tannan, Mihara-cho, Minamikawachi-Gun, Osaka, Japan Tel (0723)61-:300   Specifications are subject to change without notice. Printed in Japan Sep. '87 Code No. 59030169

SunTour Cantilever Brake

SUNTOUR
CANTILEVER BRAKE SUNTOUR
Model:CT-XC10, Code No.62699911 (SE Mechanism)

INSTRUCTION
MANUAL

Specifications are subject to change without notice.
Printed in Japan Nov. '88
Code No.59030211

Caution: The XC-9000 "SE" canti-brakes are made for use as rear brakes <u>only</u>, and are not designed for use as front brakes.

1 Apply a light coat of grease to the braze-on studs before installing the cantis. Use the sequence shown in figure 1 to assemble the cantilever assemblies onto the braze-on studs, making sure not to reverse the male helixes. Lightly tighten the mounting bolts with a 5mm allen wrench. Do not overtighten the arms should be free to pivot fully without rattling on the studs.

This will facilitate shoe positioning in step 2.

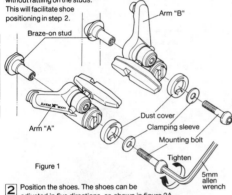

Figure 1

2 Position the shoes. The shoes can be adjusted in five directions, as shown in figure 2A.

Note: the plastic shoe grip cover encircling the shoe's post and the eyebolt is designed to grip the shoe during adjustment and prevent unwanted movement before the shoe mounting hardware has been tightened. This makes precise adjustments simpler.

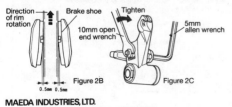

Position the shoes as shown in figure 2B. Each shoe should have enough toe-in to leave 1/2mm of clearance at the trailing end of the shoe as the leading end just begins to touch the rim (note direction of rim rotation). When you're satisfied with the shoe position, tighten the shoe mounting hardware using a 5mm allen wrench and a 10mm open end or box wrench. (Figure 2C) The shoe grip cover will hold the shoe so both your hands can be free for tightening the hardware.

Figure 2B   Figure 2C

MAEDA INDUSTRIES, LTD.
97 Tannan, Mihara-cho, Minamikawachi-Gun, Osaka, Japan Tel:(0723)61-1300

3 Loosen the mounting bolts, and rotate each arm away from the rim until there is 1/4" (6mm) of clearance between each shoe and the rim. Then, holding each arm in position, tighten each 5mm allen mounting bolt to a torque of between 80 and 90 kgf/cm.

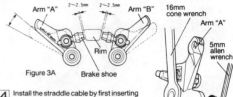

Figure 3A   Brake shoe

4 Install the straddle cable by first inserting the cable head into the cable head socket of arm "A", and then threading the other end of the cable through the cable clamp assembly on arm "B". Shorten the straddle cable until each segment is at right angles to the arm it's connected to (figure 4)* and each shoe is between 2mm and 2.5mm away from the rim (figure 3B.)

Figure 3B   Tighten

* During this operation, keep the straddle cable tight by pulling it upwards at its center with one hand, and adjusting its length with the other.

When the straddle cable is the correct length, tighten the cable clamp assembly on arm "B", and trim and cap the exposed end. Then, install the straddle cable hanger onto the main cable, and clamp it high enough along the main cable to allow each shoe to return to between 2mm and 2.5mm away from the rim.
Trim and cap the main cable.

Figure 4

If necessary, use the right-angle gauge in this manual to determine the best cable/arm angle. Use the ridge along the leading face of the brake arm as the reference for the right angle gauge. Mechanically, this "high rise" canti brake design is most effective when the straddle cable is pulling at right angles (90 to 100 degrees) to each arm. You may shorten or lengthen the straddle cable as you wish, but this will slightly diminish the efficiency of the brake.

5 Squeeze the brake lever a few times to be certain that your adjustments are stable.

6 To remove the rear wheel, squeeze the brake shoes against the rim to allow enough slack at the straddle cable to remove its cable head from its socket in arm "A". When the cable head is free, pivot the brake arms away from the wheel.

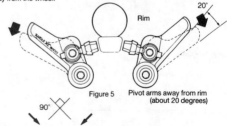

Figure 5   Pivot arms away from rim (about 20 degrees)

SunTour Exage Shift/Brake Lever

SERVICE INSTRUCTIONS

Before use, read these instructions carefully, and follow them for correct use.

Shifting Lever
SL-M451-A
SL-M451-B
SL-M452-A

Brake Lever
BL-M451

EXAGE

Note

The following products should be used together for the Shimano Index System (SIS) function.
- Shifting Lever............SL-M451/SL-M452
- Rear Derailleur..........RD-M450
- Freehub, Freewheel...FH-RM50/HB-RA50/CS-1000/MF-Z012 (6 speeds)
- Chain......................Shimano UG chain
- Outer Cable..............Shimano SIS-SP cable

The following products should be used together for the Shimano Linear Response (SLR).
- Brake Lever..............BL-M451
- Brake.......................BR-M454
- Outer Cable..............Shimano outer cable casing with liner

Shifting lever installation

Type A (unified with brake lever)

Type B (separate type)

Tightening torque: 25 ~ 30 kgfcm

Installation of the brake lever and cable

Clamp bolt tightening torque: 30 kgfcm

6-mm lock nut

Lever cover

Adjustment bolt
Adjustment nut

Outer guide hole

Inner end

Inner end adapter

① Insert the inner cable through the adjustment bolt and nut, then assemble the inner end through the outer guide hole.
② Hook the inner end on the inner end adapter.

Note: Check to be sure that the adjustment nut is securely seated in the outer guide hole.

The use of 1.6-mm inner cable and 5-mm outer casing is standard.

■ Turn the width adjustment bolt to the preferred brake width.

Width adjustment bolt

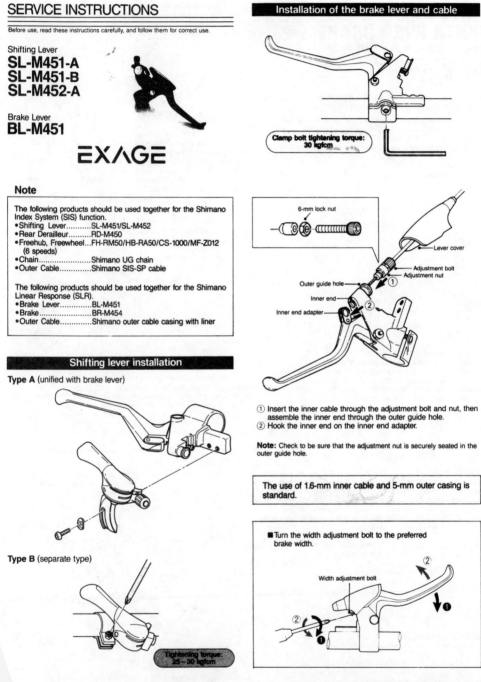

Please note: Specifications are subject to change for improvement without notice. (English)

SHIMANO AMERICAN CORPORATION   SHIMANO (EUROPA) GmbH.   SHIMANO (SINGAPORE) PTE. LTD.   SHIMANO INDUSTRIAL CO.,LTD.
Shimano Drive, Irvine, California U.S.A. 92718 Tel. (714) 951-5003   Im Hülsenfeld 13 4010 Hilden, West Germany Tel. 02103-5005-0   No. 20, Benoi Sector, Jurong Town, Singapore 2262 Tel. 2654777   3-77 Oimatsucho, Sakai, Osaka, Japan Tel. (0722) 23-3243

©Jul. 1988 by Shimano Co., Ltd. R-47 XBC SZK Printed in Japan.

Shimano Shift/Brake Lever

SERVICE INSTRUCTIONS

Before use, read these instructions carefully, and follow them for correct use.

Shifting Lever
SL-M453

Brake Lever
BL-M451

Installation of the brake lever and cable

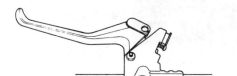

Clamp bolt tightening torque:
30 kgfcm

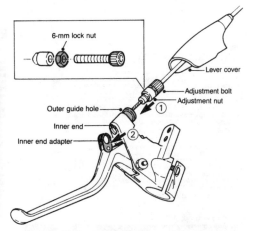

① Insert the inner cable through the adjustment bolt and nut, then assemble the inner end through the outer guide hole.
② Hook the inner end on the inner end adapter.

Note: Check to be sure that the adjustment nut is securely seated in the outer guide hole.

Note

The following products should be used together for the Shimano Index System (SIS) function.
- Shifting Lever............SL-M453
- Rear Derailleur..........RD-M452
- Freehub, Freewheel...FH-M452/CS-MT62
  (7 speeds)
- Chain.......................CN-MT62
- Outer Cable...............Shimano SIS-SP cable

The following products should be used together for the Shimano Linear Response (SLR).
- Brake Lever..............BL-M451
- Brake.......................BR-M454/BR-M453/BR-M452
- Outer Cable...............Shimano outer cable casing with liner

The use of 1.6-mm inner cable and 5-mm outer casing is standard.

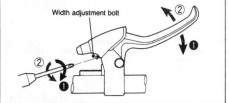

■Turn the width adjustment bolt to the preferred brake width.

Shifting lever installation

The brake lever and shifting lever are the unified type.

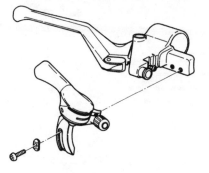

Please note: Specifications are subject to change for improvement without notice. (English)

SHIMANO AMERICAN CORPORATION   SHIMANO (EUROPA) GmbH.
One Shimano Drive, Irvine, California U.S.A. 92718 Tel. (714) 951-5003   Im Hulsenfeld 13 4010 Hilden, West Germany Tel. 02103-5005-0

SHIMANO (SINGAPORE) PTE. LTD.   SHIMANO INDUSTRIAL CO.,LTD.
No. 20, Benoi Sector, Jurong Town, Singapore 2262 Tel. 2654777   3-77 Oimatsucho, Sakai, Osaka, Japan Tel. (0722) 23-3243

© Jul. 1988 by Shimano Co., Ltd. R-57 XBC SZK Printed in Japan

Shimano Rear Derailleur

SERVICE INSTRUCTIONS

RD-M735
RD-M650 Rear Derailleur
RD-M550

Before use, read these instructions carefully, and follow them for correct use.

Capacity

Type	Total capacity	Rear smallest sprocket	Rear largest sprocket
Long cage (RD-M550)	36T or less	12T	28T~30T
Super long cage (RD-M735/ RD-M650/ RD-M550)	38T or less	12T	28T~32T

Note: The above capacity is the value when the B-tension adjustment bolt is completely tightened.

Note

- If used as STI, be sure to use the following combination:
  - STI (Shifting lever).................ST-M090/ST-M070/ST-M060/ SL-M732/SL-MT62
  - Rear derailleur.......................RD-M735/RD-M650/RD-M550
  - Freehub................................FH-M732/FH-M650/FH-M550
  - Cassette sprocket (7-speed)......CS-HG90/CS-HG70
  - Chain...................................CN-HG90/CN-HG70
  - Outer cable............................Shimano SIS-SP cable
- Because the high cable resistance of a frame with internal cable guides would impair the SIS function, this type of frame should not be used.
- RD-M735, RD-M650 and RD-M550 cannot be used in combination with the Dura Ace shifting lever.
- The tension of the guide spring can be set to any one of three steps. If a higher return force for the rear derailleur is necessary because riding conditions are poor, set to the STRONG setting. If the riding conditions are very good, a lighter, smoother lever operation feeling can be obtained by setting to the WEAK position.
- The setting is strong at the ○ mark.

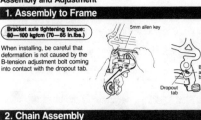

Assembly and Adjustment

1. Assembly to Frame

Bracket axle tightening torque:
80—100 kgfcm (70—85 in.lbs.)

When installing, be careful that deformation is not caused by the B-tension adjustment bolt coming into contact with the dropout tab.

2. Chain Assembly

Largest gear   Largest gear
Chain
Add 2 links (with chain tightened)

3. Stroke Adjustment and Cable Connection

1. Top adjustment
Turn the top adjustment bolt to adjust so that, looking from the rear, the guide pulley is below the outer line of the top gear.

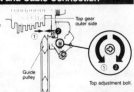

---

2. Inner cable connection
Connect the inner cable to the rear derailleur and, after the pre-stretch as shown in the figure, reconnect to the rear derailleur.

Pull.

Note: Be sure the inner cable is securely in the groove.

Groove

3. Low adjustment
Shift to lowest gear and turn the low adjustment bolt to adjust so that the guide pulley moves to a position directly below the low gear.

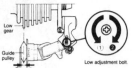

4. How to Use B-Tension Adjustment Bolt

Mount the chain on the chainwheel's smallest gear and the freewheel's largest gear, and turn the crank backward. Then turn the B-tension adjustment bolt to adjust the guide pulley as close to the gear as possible but not so close that it touches. Next, set the freewheel to the smallest gear and repeat the above to make sure the pulley does not touch.

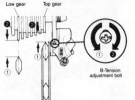

5. STI Adjustment

1. Operate the shifting lever to move the chain from the top gear to the 2nd gear.
   - If the chain will **not move to the 2nd gear,** turn the cable adjusting barrel to increase the tension.....① **(counter clockwise)**
   - If the chain **moves past the 2nd gear,** decrease the tension.....② **(clockwise)**

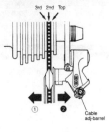

2. Next with the chain on the 2nd gear, increase the inner cable tension ① while turning the crank forward. Stop turning the cable adjusting barrel **just before the chain makes noise against the 3rd gear.** This completes the adjustment.

For the best STI performance, lubrication is recommended for all power-transmission parts. The optimum oil is dry molybdenum oil or a similar oil.

Please note: specifications are subject to change for improvement without notice. (English)

SHIMANO AMERICAN CORPORATION
One Shimano Drive, Irvine, California U.S.A. 92718 Tel: (714) 951 5003
SHIMANO (EUROPA) GmbH.
Im Hülsenholz 13 4010 Hilden, West Germany Tel: 02103 5005 0

SHIMANO (SINGAPORE) PTE. LTD.
No. 20, Benoi Sector, Jurong Town Singapore 2262 Tel: 2654777
SHIMANO INDUSTRIAL CO.LTD.
3-77 Oimatsucho, Sakai, Osaka Japan Tel: (0722) 23 3243

© Jun. 1989 by Shimano Co., Ltd. T-8 XBC SZK Printed in Japan.

Shimano Front Derailleur

SERVICE INSTRUCTIONS

FD-M735   FD-M400
FD-M650   FD-M300
FD-M500

Before use, read these instructions carefully, and follow them for correct use.

Note:
- This front derailleur is for front chainwheel triple gear use only. It cannot be used with the double gear, because the shifting performance is not good.
- For the chain, be sure to use only the Shimano narrow-type chain. The wide-type chain cannot be used.

Specifications

Capacity (front gear tooth difference)	AL specifications *1	Round gear	8T ~ 26T
		CR-BP15	8T ~ 22T
		SG gear	8T ~ 22T
	HS specifications *2	Round gear	5T ~ 26T
		CR-BP15	5T ~ 22T
		SG gear	5T ~ 22T
Installation band diameter	Band type	⌀28.00 ~ ⌀28.60mm (1-3/32" ~ 1-1/8")	
	EC type	⌀31.8mm (1-1/14"), ⌀34.9mm (1-3/8")	
Stroke	Band type	34 ~ 54mm (1-11/32" ~ 2-1/8")	
	EC type	⌀31.8mm	35 ~ 55mm (1-3/8" ~ 2-5/32")
		⌀34.9mm	36 ~ 56mm (1-19/32" ~ 2-1/2")

*1: (if difference between top and middle is 8 teeth or more)
*2: (if difference between top and middle is 5 teeth or more)

Installation to the frame

1. For the Biopace, set so the crank comes to the position of an imaginary line extended from the seat tube.

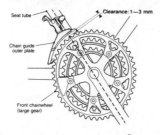

Clearance: 1—3 mm
Seat tube
Chain guide outer plate
Front chainwheel (large gear)

2. The outside surface Ⓐ of the chain guide should be directly above and parallel to the large gear.
3. Secure by using a 5mm allen key.

Tightening torque:
60 kgfcm (43 in.lbs.)

Front chainwheel (large gear)
Chainguide
Ⓐ

Adjustment and cable securing

4. Low adjustment
Set so that the clearance between the chain guide inner plate and the chain is 1—1.5 mm.

Chain position

Largest gear   Smallest gear

Low adjustment bolt
Ⓐ Ⓑ

Chain guide inner plate
Chain

5. Cable attachment
While pulling the cable forcefully, tighten the holding bolt at a torque of 50 kgfcm. Use a 5-mm allen key to secure.

6. Top adjustment
Set the chain guide outer plate to the smallest gap at which the chain guide does not contact the chain.

Chain position

Smallest gear   Largest gear

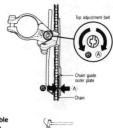

Top adjustment bolt
Ⓑ Ⓐ
Chain guide outer plate
Chain

7. Tension adjustment of the STI cable
1. After taking up the initial slack in the cable, reattach to the front derailleur.

Pull

2. Set the chain onto the largest gear of the rear sprocket, and shift the front chainwheel from the smallest gear to the intermediate gear to the largest gear.

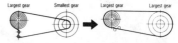

Largest gear   Smallest gear   Largest gear   Largest gear

3. Next, shift the front chainwheel from the largest gear to the intermediate gear, and then adjust, by using the outer cable adjustment bolt of the shifting lever, so that there is the least possible clearance between the chain guide inner plate and the chain, but without them contacting each other.

Chain position

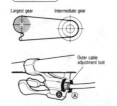

Largest gear   Intermediate gear

Outer cable adjustment bolt
Ⓑ Ⓐ
Chain guide inner bolt
Chain

8. Trouble shooting chart
After completion of 1—7, move the shift lever to check the shifting. (This also applies if shifting becomes difficult during use.)

If the chain falls to the crank side	Tighten the top adjustment bolt clockwise (about 1/4 turn).
If shifting is difficult from the intermediate gear to the large gear	Loosen the top adjustment bolt counter-clockwise (about 1/8 turn).
If shifting is difficult from the intermediate gear to the small gear	Loosen the low adjustment bolt counter-clockwise (about 1/4 turn).
If there is interference of the chain and front derailleur inner plate at the largest gear of the front chain wheel	Tighten the top adjustment bolt clockwise (about 1/8 turn).
If there is interference of the chain and front derailleur outer plate at the largest gear of the front chain wheel	Loosen the top adjustment bolt counter-clockwise (1/8 turn).
If the intermediate gear is skipped when shifting from the largest gear	Loosen the outer cable adjustment bolt counterclockwise (1 or 2 turns). ★
If there is interference of the chain and front derailleur inner plate when, at the intermediate gear position, the rear chainwheel is shifted to the largest gear.	Tighten the outer cable adjustment bolt clockwise (1 or 2 turns). ★
If the chain falls to the bottom bracket side	Tighten the low adjustment bolt clockwise (1/2 turn).

Note: If use is not as STI, the following steps are not necessary: 7. Tension adjustment of the STI cable, and 8. Trouble shooting chart ★

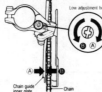
SHIMANO

Please note: specifications are subject to change for improvement without notice. (English)

SHIMANO AMERICAN CORPORATION
One Shimano Drive, Irvine, California U.S.A. 92718 Tel. (714) 951-5003

SHIMANO (EUROPA) GmbH.
Im Huisenfeld 13 4010 Hilden, West Germany Tel. 02103-5005-0

SHIMANO (SINGAPORE) PTE. LTD.
No. 20, Benoi Sector, Jurong Town, Singapore 2262 Tel. 2654777

SHIMANO INDUSTRIAL CO.,LTD.
3-77 Oimatsucho, Sakai, Osaka, Japan Tel. (0722) 23-3243

May. 1989 by Shimano Co., Ltd. T-15 XBC IZM Printed in Japan.

Shimano U-Brake

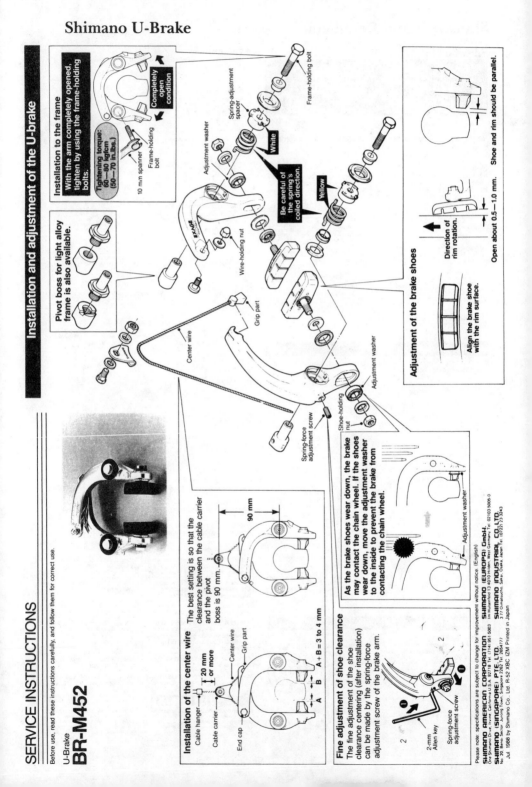

Shimano Deore II Cantilever Brake

SERVICE INSTRUCTIONS

Before use, read these instructions carefully, and follow them for correct use.

Cantilever Brake
BR-MT62
Brake Lever
BL-MT62
(normal type)
BL-MT63
(two-finger type)

SHIMANO
DEORE II

Weight
- BR-MT62: 172g
- BL-MT62: 340g (left/right pair)
- BL-MT63: 272g (left/right pair)

Installation of the brake lever and cable

Pass the inner cable through the outer end cap and the outer casing; then align the lever's slit and the slit of the holding nut and the outer adjustment bolt, and install the brake cable.

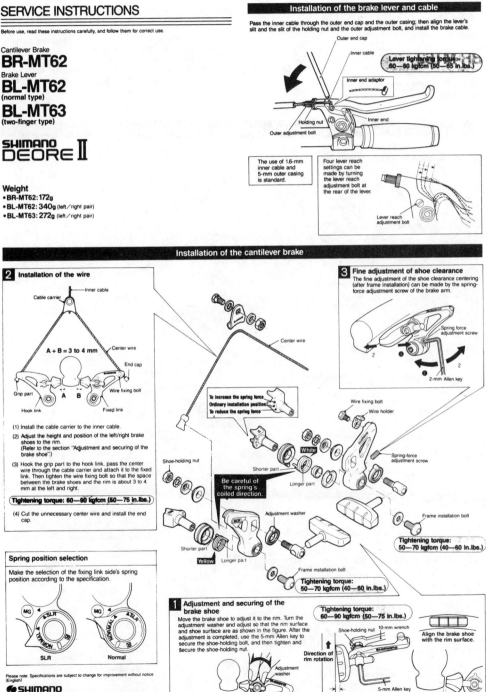

Outer end cap
Inner cable
Lever tightening torque:
60—80 kgfcm (50—65 in.lbs.)
Inner end adaptor
Holding nut
Inner end
Outer adjustment bolt

The use of 1.6-mm inner cable and 5-mm outer casing is standard.

Four lever reach settings can be made by turning the lever reach adjustment bolt at the rear of the lever.

Lever reach adjustment bolt

Installation of the cantilever brake

2 Installation of the wire

Cable carrier
Inner cable
Center wire
A + B = 3 to 4 mm
End cap
Wire fixing bolt
Grip part
A B
Hook link
Fixed link

(1) Install the cable carrier to the inner cable.
(2) Adjust the height and position of the left/right brake shoes to the rim.
(Refer to the section "Adjustment and securing of the brake shoe".)
(3) Hook the grip part to the hook link, pass the center wire through the cable carrier and attach it to the fixed link. Then tighten the wire fixing bolt so that the space between the brake shoes and the rim is about 3 to 4 mm at the left and right.

Tightening torque: 60—90 kgfcm (50—75 in.lbs.)

(4) Cut the unnecessary center wire and install the end cap.

Spring position selection

Make the selection of the fixing link side's spring position according to the specification.

MG SLR MG SLR
TENSION NORMAL
SLR Normal

3 Fine adjustment of shoe clearance
The fine adjustment of the shoe clearance centering (after frame installation) can be made by the spring-force adjustment screw of the brake arm.

Spring force adjustment screw
2-mm Allen key

Center wire

To increase the spring force
Ordinary installation position
To reduce the spring force

Wire fixing bolt
Wire holder
Spring-force adjustment screw
Shoe-holding nut
Shorter part
White
Longer part
Be careful of the spring's coiled direction.
Adjustment washer
Frame installation bolt
Shorter part
Yellow Longer part
Frame installation bolt

Tightening torque: 50—70 kgfcm (40—60 in.lbs.)

Tightening torque: 50—70 kgfcm (40—60 in.lbs.)

1 Adjustment and securing of the brake shoe

Move the brake shoe to adjust it to the rim. Turn the adjustment washer and adjust so that the rim surface and shoe surface are as shown in the figure. After the adjustment is completed, use the 5-mm Allen key to secure the shoe-holding bolt, and then tighten and secure the shoe-holding nut.

Tightening torque: 60—90 kgfcm (50—75 in.lbs.)

Shoe-holding nut
10-mm wrench
Align the brake shoe with the rim surface.
Direction of rim rotation
Adjustment washer
5-mm Allen key
Open about 0.5—1.0 mm.
Shoe and rim should be parallel.

Please note: Specifications are subject to change for improvement without notice (English)

SHIMANO

SHIMANO AMERICAN CORPORATION   SHIMANO (SINGAPORE) PTE. LTD.
SHIMANO (EUROPA) GmbH.   SHIMANO INDUSTRIAL CO.,LTD.

Jul. 1988 by Shimano Co., Ltd. R-81 XBC SZK Printed in Japan

Shimano Exage Cantilever Brake

SERVICE INSTRUCTIONS

Before use, read these instructions carefully, and follow them for correct use.

Cantilever Brake

BR-M350
EXAGE

The following products should be used together for the Shimano Linear Response (SLR).
- Cantilever Brake......BR-M350
- Brake Lever............BL-M350/BL-M450/BL-M451
- Outer Cable...........Shimano outer cable casing with liner

Installation of the cantilever brake

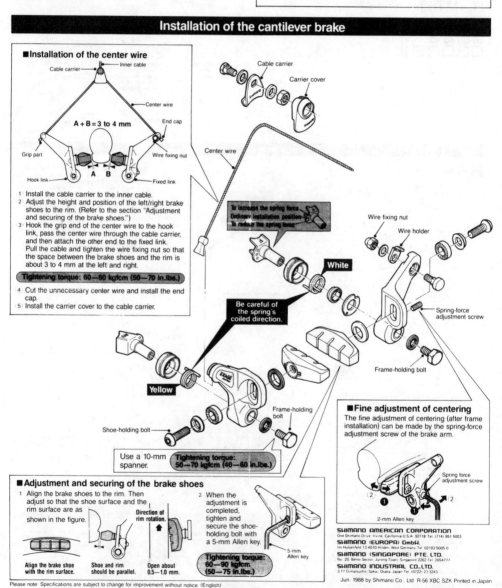

■Installation of the center wire

A + B = 3 to 4 mm

1 Install the cable carrier to the inner cable.
2 Adjust the height and position of the left/right brake shoes to the rim. (Refer to the section "Adjustment and securing of the brake shoes.")
3 Hook the grip end of the center wire to the hook link, pass the center wire through the cable carrier, and then attach the other end to the fixed link. Pull the cable and tighten the wire fixing nut so that the space between the brake shoes and the rim is about 3 to 4 mm at the left and right.

Tightening torque: 60—80 kgfcm (50—70 in.lbs.)

4 Cut the unnecessary center wire and install the end cap.
5 Install the carrier cover to the cable carrier.

To increase the spring force.
Ordinary installation position.
To reduce the spring force.

Be careful of the spring's coiled direction.

White

Yellow

Use a 10-mm spanner.

Tightening torque: 50—70 kgfcm (40—60 in.lbs.)

■Adjustment and securing of the brake shoes

1 Align the brake shoes to the rim. Then adjust so that the shoe surface and the rim surface are as shown in the figure.

Direction of rim rotation.

2 When the adjustment is completed, tighten and secure the shoe-holding bolt with a 5-mm Allen key.

Align the brake shoe with the rim surface.   Shoe and rim should be parallel.   Open about 0.5—1.0 mm.

Tightening torque: 60—90 kgfcm (50—75 in.lbs.)

■Fine adjustment of centering

The fine adjustment of centering (after frame installation) can be made by the spring-force adjustment screw of the brake arm.

Spring force adjustment screw

2-mm Allen key

SHIMANO AMERICAN CORPORATION
One Shimano Drive, Irvine, California U.S.A. 92718 Tel. (714) 951 5003
SHIMANO (EUROPA) GmbH.
Im Hulsenfeld 13 4010 Hilden, West Germany Tel. 02103 5005 0
SHIMANO (SINGAPORE) PTE. LTD.
No. 20, Benoi Sector, Jurong Town, Singapore 2262 Tel. 2654777
SHIMANO INDUSTRIAL CO. LTD.
3-77 Oimatsucho, Sakai, Osaka, Japan Tel. (0722) 23 3243

Please note: Specifications are subject to change for improvement without notice. (English)

Jun. 1988 by Shimano Co., Ltd. R-56 XBC SZK Printed in Japan

Dia-Compe Cantilever Brakes

INSTALLATION OF DIA-COMPE CANTILEVER BRAKES 984/984D

1. Brazing Pivot Studs (980.7 & 980.8)

The pivot studs should be brazed on the front forks and seat stays in a position which allows the brake shoes to contact the rim correctly. in general, the location is approximately 255 mm from the front fork ends and approximately 248 mm from the seat stay end plates when using a RM-20 (26×1.50) rim.

The distance is measured from the center of the fork ends as shown in illustrations a and b. However, the dimensions may vary depending on the size of front forks, seat stays and rims.

> **IMPORTANT: Be sure the riveted section of pivot stud is brazed before attaching to the frame.**

BRAZED-ON LOCATION FOR 984/984D

RIM OUTSIDE DIAMETER	RIM WIDTH	A	B	C			D		
				MED	MIN ~ MAX		MED	MIN ~ MAX	
575	27	255	248	80	74 ~ 86		85	80 ~ 90	
575	23	255	248	77	72 ~ 82		81	76 ~ 86	
575	32	255	248	83	78 ~ 88		91	86 ~ 96	

C = When Shoe Adjustment Washer is in Shoe Nut side.

D = When Shoe Adjustment Washer is in Brakeshoe Pad side.

RIVETED SECTION

2. Installation to Frame

a. Apply grease (lubricant) on the contacting surfaces of the frame bosses and the brake arm attaching area.
b. Note that spring adjustment direction for right and left brake arms is different. (see Fig. 1)
c. Be sure that spring is securely attached in the hole on the brake arm, spring cover and Spring Tension Adjuster.
Install brake arm, spring cover and spring tension adjuster on to the boss with attaching bolt.
Note: Do not set any spring tension at this stage.
Tightening a torque of 60 to 80 kgf·cm

3. Adjusting and Fixing Brakeshoes

a. Brake arm should have free movement when adjusting brakeshoe.
b. Facing the shue surface to the rim, set it as shown right in Fig. 2.
c. Hold the shoe with hand and tighten the brake nut with 6 mm Allen⁻Key wrench. Tightening torque should be 70 to 90 kgf·cm.
d. Use the brakeshoe adjustment washer in the shoe side when the shoe needs to be closer to the rim.

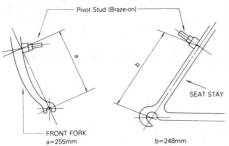

FRONT   REAR

Pivot Stud (Braze-on)

SEAT STAY

FRONT FORK
a=255mm   b=248mm

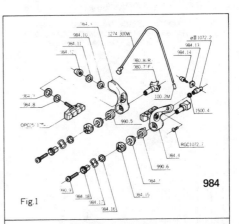

Fig.1

984

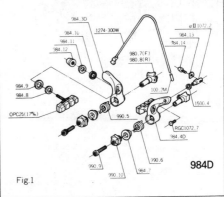

Fig.1

984D

4. Connecting to Braking Cable

a. Attach the braking cable to the straddle cable bridge.
b. Set the straddle cable as in Fig. 4, and adjust the shoe-rim leaving clearance of 1.5 mm on both sides.
c. Tighten the straddle cable with the cable fixing bolt using a 5mm allen key wrench.
   The tightening torque should be 50 to 70 kgf·cm.
d. Cut off the excess straddle cable and attach the cable cap.

5. Tuning the shoe clearance and spring tension

a. When the left side (a in the Fig. 4) is greater than b, turn the spring tension adjuster in the A or C direction.
   When the right side b is greater than a turn the spring tension adjuster in the B or D direction.
   Use a 13 mm (984D) open wrench or 19 mm (984).
b. When spring tension must be tightened, turn the spring tension adjuster to B or C. When loosening, turn to A or D.
c. Tighten the attaching bolt with a torque of 60 to 80 kgf·cm.

■ IT IS IMPORTANT TO CHECK THE BRAKE ALIGNMENT AGAINST THE RIM PERIODICALLY IN ORDER TO MAINTAIN HIGH PERFORMANCES OF DIA-COMPE BRAKES.

984D

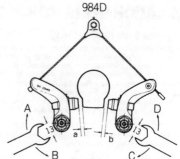

Fig.4

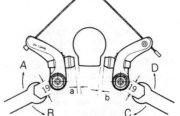

984

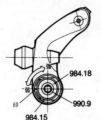

984.18
990.9
984.15

Fig.5

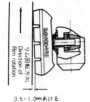

0.5~1.0mmあける

Fig.2

6mm
Allen Key

Fig.3

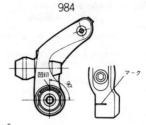

マーク

Fig.6

DIA-COMPE CANTILEVER BRAKES 984/984D

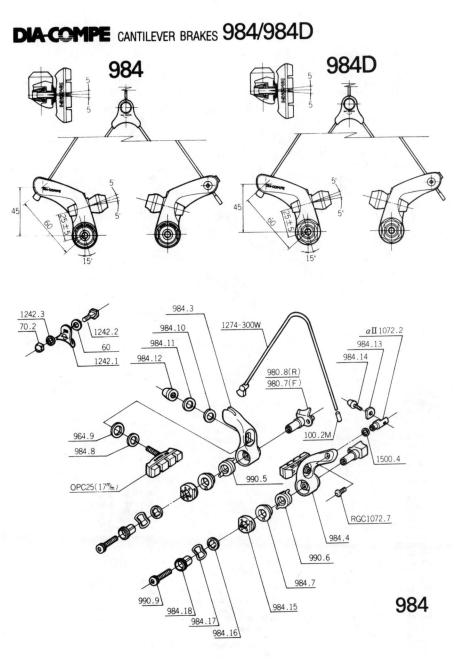

984

984D

1242.3
70.2
60
1242.2
1242.1
984.3
984.10
984.11
984.12
1274-300W
980.8(R)
980.7(F)
αⅡ1072.2
984.13
984.14
984.9
984.8
100.2M
1500.4
OPC25(17mm)
990.5
RGC1072.7
984.4
990.6
990.9
984.18
984.17
984.16
984.7
984.15

984

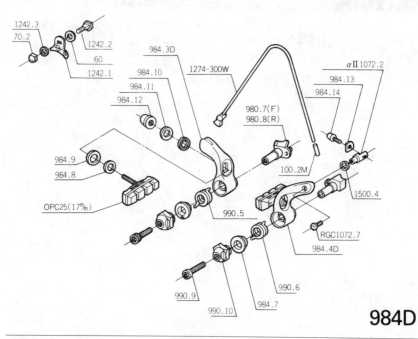

984D

Code No.	Catalog No.	Description	品　　名
060527	OPC25	Brake shoe (17mm bolt)	舟ゴム付
160224	60	Washer	座金
150409	70.2	Acorn nut	袋ナット
240312	100.2M	Aluminum end cap for cable	アルミインナーキャップ
024107	984.3	Stirrup for right (984)	右用アーチ本体
024108	984.3D	Stirrup for right (984D)	右用アーチ本体
024106	984.4	Stirrup for left (984)	左用アーチ本体
024104	984.4D	Stirrup for left (984D)	左用アーチ本体
160825	984.7	Spring cover	バネカバー
050615	984.8	Washer convex	角度調整座金
050617	984.9	Washer concave	角度調整座金
050425	984.10	Washer serrated	ローレット座金
050619	984.11	Washer convex	角度調整座金
150238	984.12K	Nut black (984)	舟ゴム取付用ナット
150237	984.12	Nut (984D)	舟ゴム取付用ナット
160622	984.13	Cable binding plate	ワイヤー止座金
120523	984.14	Cable fixing bolt	ワイヤー止ボルト
260122	984.15	Spring adjuster	ラチェット爪後
260121	984.16	Ratchet	ラチェット爪前
160730	984.17	Wave washer	波座金
260304	984.18	Sleeve	ラチェット取付座金
040439	990.5	Spring for stirrup, right (gold)	右用バネ（黄）
040440	990.6	Spring for stirrup, left (silver)	左用バネ（白）
600106	990.9	Bolt for stirrup pivot	アーチ取付ボルト
050742	990.10	Spring adjuster	アーチ固定座金
120314	αⅡ1072.2	Quick release stud	クイックレリース用ダルマネジ
120508	RGC1072.7	Bolt	ボルト
090217	1242.1	Straddle cable bridge main body	吊金具本体のみ
120203	1242.2	Cable clamp bolt	インナー止ボルト
160305	1242.3	Cable clamp	座金
119952	1274-300W	Straddle cable 300mm braided	アーチワイヤー300㎜
630302	1500.4	Washer	座金

INSTALLATION OF DIA-COMPE CANTILEVER BRAKES   986

❋PLEASE READ INSTRUCTIONS CAREFULLY BEFORE USE.

1. Brazing Pivot Studs (982.7-III & 982.8-III)

The pivot studs should be brazed on the front forks and seat stays in a position which allows the brake shoes to contact the rim correctly. in general, the location is approximately 255mm from the front fork ends and approximately 253mm from the seat stay end plates when using a 7×26×1.75 rim. The distance is measured from the center of the fork ends as shown in illustrations a and b. However, the dimensions may vary depending on the size of front forks, seat stays and rims.

2. Installation to Frame

a. Apply grease (lubricant) on the contacting surfaces of the frame bosses and the brake arm attaching area.
b. Note that spring adjustment direction for right and left brake arms is different. (see Fig.C)
c. Be sure that spring is securely attached in the hole on the brake arm, spring cover and Spring Tension Adjuster.
   Install brake arm, spring cover and spring tension adjuster on to the boss with attaching bolt.
   Note: Do not set any spring tension at this stage.
   Tightening a torque of 60 to 80 kgf·cm

3. Adjusting and Fixing Brakeshoes

a. Brake arm should have free movement when adjusting brakeshoe. Brakeshoe has right-use and left-use — This installation must be careful. See Fig. D
b. Facing the shoe surface to the rim, set it as shown in Fig. E.
c. Hold the shoe by hand, and tighten the brakeshoe nut with 6mm Allen-key wrench. See Fig. D.
   Proper tightening torque: 70 ~ 90 kgf·cm.

BRAZED-ON LOCATION FOR 986

RIM OUTSIDE DIAMETER	RIM WIDTH	A	B	C	
				MED	MIN~MAX
575	27	255	253	77	70~84
575	23	255	253	73	66~80
575	32	255	253	82	75~89

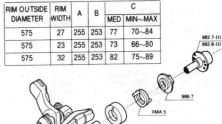
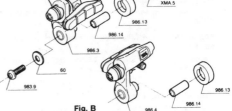
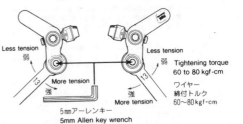

982.7-III
982.8-III
986.7
XMA.5
986.13
986.14
986.3
60
983.9
986.13
986.14
986.4

Fig. B

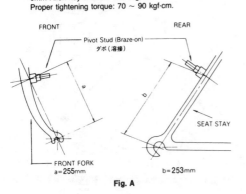

FRONT   REAR

Pivot Stud (Braze-on)
ダボ（溶接）

a

b

SEAT STAY

FRONT FORK
a=255mm

b=253mm

Fig. A

Less tension
弱   Less tension
                            弱   Tightening torque
13   13   60 to 80 kgf-cm
More tension   ワイヤー
強   強   締付トルク
            More tension   60~80kgf-cm
5mmアーレンキー
5mm Allen key wrench

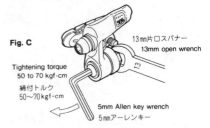

Fig. C

                                        13mm片ロスパナー
                                        13mm open wrench
Tightening torque   13
50 to 70 kgf-cm
締付トルク
50~70kgf-cm
                            5mm Allen key wrench
                            5mmアーレンキー

> Note: The brake shoe pad should be angled so the front portion contacts the rim prior to the rest of the pad's surface. See Fig.E. The illustration shows front assembly.

4. Connecting to Braking Cable (1276-300W)

a. Attach the braking cable to the straddle cable bridge.
b. Set the straddle cable as in Fig.F, and adjust the shoe-rim leaving clearance of 1.5mm on both sides.
c. Tighten the straddle cable with the cable anchor bolt (986.15). The tightening torque should be 60 to 80 kgf·cm.
d. Cut off the excess straddle cable and attach the cable cap. (100.2)

5. Adjustment of the Clearance Between Brake Shoe and Rim

① Loosen the acorn nut (70.2) of No.1242 Straddle Cable Bridge, and adjust the straddle cable. Then, retighten the acorn nut.

② Tuning Spring Tension

a. Both right and left brake arms have spring tension adjustment system.
b. Your favorable spring tension can be adjustable.
c. First one side of two brake arms' spring tension should be adjusted, then the other side should be done. See Fig. C. Brake Lever operating force can be adjusted to 0.5 ~ 3.0 kgf.

■ IT IS IMPORTANT TO CHECK THE BRAKE ALIGHNMENT AGAINST THE RIM PERIODICALLY IN ORDER TO MAINTAIN HIGH PERFORMANCES OF DIA-COMPE BRAKES.

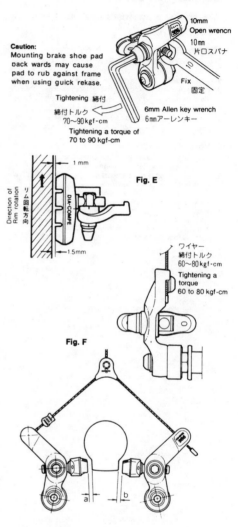

Caution:
Mounting brake shoe pad back wards may cause pad to rub against frame when using quick rekase.

Tightening 締付
締付トルク
70〜90kgf·cm
Tightening a torque of 70 to 90 kgf·cm

10mm Open wrencn
10mm 片口スパナ
Fix 固定
6mm Allen key wrench
6mmアーレンキー

Direction of Rim rotation
リム回転方向

1 mm
1.5mm

Fig. E

ワイヤー
締付トルク
60〜80kgf·cm
Tightening a torque 60 to 80 kgf-cm

Fig. F

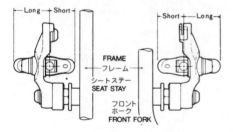

Long — Short   Short — Long

FRAME
フレーム
シートステー
SEAT STAY
フロント
ホーク
FRONT FORK

Fig. D

a   b

DIA-COMPE CANTILEVER BRAKES **986**

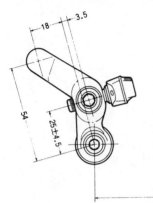

Code No.	Catalog No.	Description
025007	986.3	Stirrup for right
040455	XMA.5	Spring for stirrup, right (Gold)
160833	986.13	Spring cover
160538	986.14	Sleeve
050811	986.7	Spring adjuster
230841	982.7-III	Pivot for front stirrup
230843	982.8-III	Pivot for rear stirrup
050622	986.9	Washer for nut
050623	986.10	Washer for brake shoe
060537	986.5	Brake shoe for right
060538	986.6	Brake shoe for left
160633	986.16	Cable binding plate
150409	70.2	Acorn nut
040456	XMA.6	Spring for stirrup, left (Silver)
025015	986.4	Sterrup for left
150246	986.11	Nut
160224	60	Washer
030542	983.9	Bolt for stirrup pivot
120525	986.15	Cable anchor bolt only
070210	986.8	Eye bolt for brake shoe
160277	986.12	Washer
240312	100.2M	Aluminum end cap for cable
119964	1276-300W	Straddle cable 300mm
090217	1242.1	Straddle cable bridge only
120203	1242.2	Cable anchor bolt only
160305	1242.3	Cable clamp

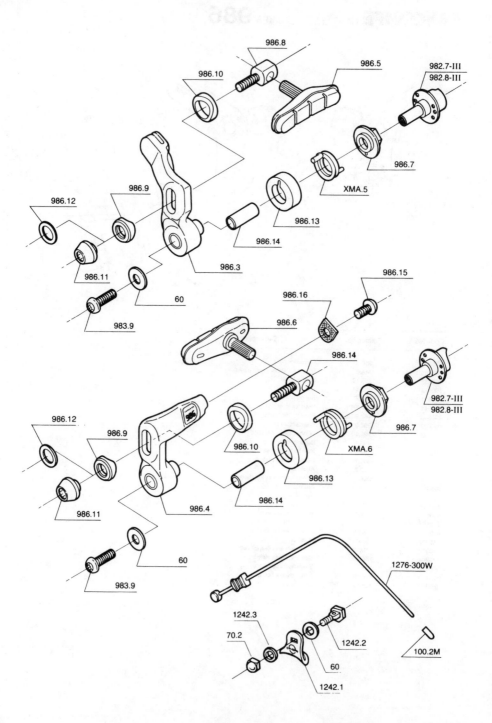

Dia-Compe Advantage 992 Brake

PLEASE READ INSTRUCTIONS CAREFULLY BEFORE USE

DIA-COMPE *Advantage 992* BRAKE

INSTALLATION INSTRUCTIONS

Specification : Weight – 243g.

Materials – Cold-forged Light Alloy (main body)
Steel   Plastic

Brakeshoe – One-piece composite shoe (OPC-11)

1 Installation to Frame

a. Apply grease (lubricant) on the contacting surfaces of the frame bosses and the brake arm attaching area.

b. Note that spring adjustment direction for right and left brake arms is different. (see Fig. 1)

c. Be sure that spring is securely attached in the hole on the brake arm, spring cover and Spring Adjuster. Then tighten the attaching bolt with 5mm Allen key wrench (supplied). Tightening torque should be 60 to 80 kgf. cm.

3 Connecting to Braking Cable (See Fig. 4)

a. Attach the braking cable to the straddle cable bridge.

b. Set the straddle cable as in Fig. 4, and adjust the shoe-rim leaving clearance of 1.5mm on both sides.

c. Tighten the straddle cable with the cable fixing nut. The tightening torque should be 50 to 70 kgf. cm.

d. Cut off the excess straddle cable and attach the cable cap.

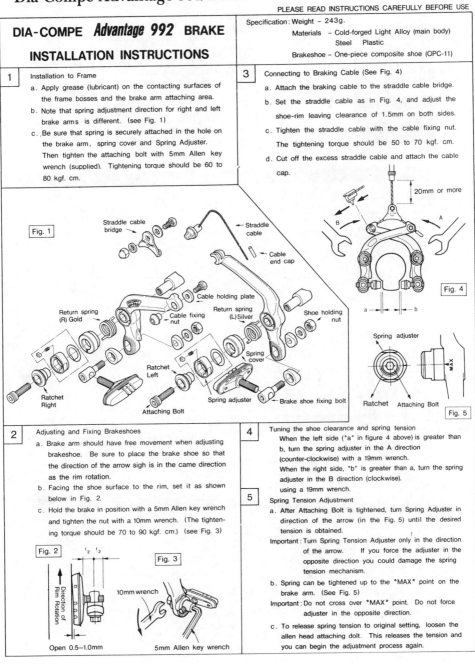

Fig. 1

Fig. 4

Fig. 5

2 Adjusting and Fixing Brakeshoes

a. Brake arm should have free movement when adjusting brakeshoe. Be sure to place the brake shoe so that the direction of the arrow sigh is in the came direction as the rim rotation.

b. Facing the shoe surface to the rim, set it as shown below in Fig. 2.

c. Hold the brake in position with a 5mm Allen key wrench and tighten the nut with a 10mm wrench. (The tightening torque should be 70 to 90 kgf. cm.) (see Fig. 3)

4 Tuning the shoe clearance and spring tension

When the left side ("a" in figure 4 above) is greater than b, turn the spring adjuster in the A direction (counter-clockwise) with a 19mm wrench. When the right side, "b" is greater than a, turn the spring adjuster in the B direction (clockwise) using a 19mm wrench.

5 Spring Tension Adjustment

a. After Attaching Bolt is tightened, turn Spring Adjuster in direction of the arrow (in the Fig. 5) until the desired tension is obtained.

Important : Turn Spring Tension Adjuster only in the direction of the arrow.   If you force the adjuster in the opposite direction you could damage the spring tension mechanism.

b. Spring can be tightened up to the "MAX" point on the brake arm. (See Fig. 5)

Important : Do not cross over "MAX" point. Do not force adjuster in the opposite direction.

c. To release spring tension to original setting, loosen the allen head attaching dolt. This releases the tension and you can begin the adjustment process again.

Shimano Freehubs

SERVICE INSTRUCTION

FH-M650
FH-M550   Freehubs
FH-HG50
FH-HG20

For proper and safe performance, read and follow these instructions
carefully.

■ Notes
• Always be sure to use the HG (Hyper Glide)
  sprocket set bearing the same group marking.
  Never use in combination with a sprocket bearing
  a different group marking.

• Freehubs (FH-M650, FH-M550, FH-HG50) for the
  HG sprockets can also be used with the former
  UG sprockets (CS-6400, CS-1000), but never use
  the HG sprockets and UG sprockets in combination.

  Note that although the FH-HG20 freehub can also
  be used with the UG sprockets, the UG sprockets
  cannot be used for the top gear.
  (For the top gear use the lock ring and top gear from the HG sprocket set.)

• For the HG sprocket, be sure to use the CN-HG70 or the CN-HG50 narrow chain.

Group marks

Installation of the HG sprocket

For each sprocket, the surface that has the group
mark should face outward and positioned so that
the triangle (▲) mark on each sprocket and the A
part (where the groove width is wide) of the
freewheel are aligned.

※ For FH-HG50 and FH-HG20, the six sprockets
  (other than top gear) are rivetted and so cannot
  be disassembled.

The groove width is wide
at one place only.   ▲ mark

Freewheel

Sprocket spacers D
(color: grey / t=3.1mm)

※ The three projections of sprocket spacers D should face toward the low side,
  and be aligned with the sprocket fixing
  bolts.

Low side   Projection

Sprocket spacer C
(color: black / t=3.3mm)

※ The three holes of sprocket spacer C
  should be aligned with the sprocket
  fixing bolts.

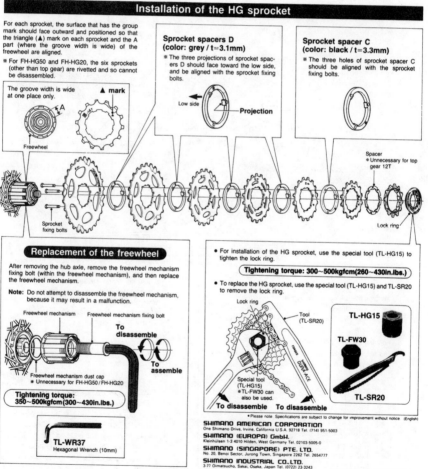

Spacer
※ Unnecessary for top
  gear 12T

Sprocket
fixing bolts

Lock ring

Replacement of the freewheel

After removing the hub axle, remove the freewheel mechanism
fixing bolt (within the freewheel mechanism), and then replace
the freewheel mechanism.

Note: Do not attempt to disassemble the freewheel mechanism,
      because it may result in a malfunction.

Freewheel mechanism   Freewheel mechanism fixing bolt

To
disassemble

To
assemble

Freewheel mechanism dust cap
※ Unnecessary for FH-HG50 / FH-HG20

Tightening torque:
350~500kgfcm(300~430in.lbs.)

TL-WR37
Hexagonal Wrench (10mm)

• For installation of the HG sprocket, use the special tool (TL-HG15) to
  tighten the lock ring.

Tightening torque: 300~500kgfcm(260~430in.lbs.)

• To replace the HG sprocket, use the special tool (TL-HG15) and TL-SR20
  to remove the lock ring.

Lock ring

Tool
(TL-SR20)

Special tool
(TL-HG15)
※ TL-FW30 can
  also be used.

To disassemble   To disassemble

TL-HG15

TL-FW30

TL-SR20

• Please note: Specifications are subject to change for improvement without notice. (English)

SHIMANO AMERICAN CORPORATION
One Shimano Drive, Irvine, California U.S.A. 92718 Tel. (714) 951-5003
SHIMANO (EUROPA) GmbH.
Kleinhülsen 1-3 4010 Hilden, West Germany Tel. 02103-5005-0
SHIMANO (SINGAPORE) PTE. LTD.
No. 20, Benoi Sector, Jurong Town, Singapore 2262 Tel. 2654777
SHIMANO INDUSTRIAL CO.,LTD.
3-77 Oimatsucho, Sakai, Osaka, Japan Tel. (0722) 23-3243

© May. 1989 by Shimano T-34 PIT SZK Printed in Japan

Shimano Front Chainwheel

SERVICE INSTRUCTION

Front Chainwheel

FC-M730	FC-MT60

SHIMANO DEORE XT   **SHIMANO DEORE**

Before use, read these instructions carefully, and follow them for correct use.

NOTE

- Bolt circle diameter:
  110mm (For Large Gear & Middle Gear)
  74mm (For Small Gear)
- Use the following bottom bracket spindle.

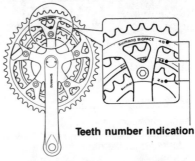

	Shell width	A	B	C	D
D-3NL	68	122.5	52	36	34.5
D-5NL	70	122.5	54	35	33.5

(Unit: mm)

Biopace Chainring Assembly

- Install the chainring with the teeth number indication to the outside and to the top as shown below.

Teeth number indication

Notes for installation of the front derailleur

- Use the front derailleur with a capacity (teeth number difference between the large gear and small gear) plus 2 teeth or more.

- Adjust the installation position of the front derailleur so that the clearance between the outer plate of the chainguide and the large gear is 1 to 3mm while the crank is in a direct line with the seat tube.

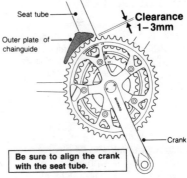

Seat tube

Clearance 1–3mm

Outer plate of chainguide

Crank

Be sure to align the crank with the seat tube.

- Please note: Specifications are subject to change for improvement whithout notice.

SHIMANO AMERICAN CORPORATION
One Shimano Drive, Irvine, California U.S.A. 92718 Tel. (714) 951-5003
SHIMANO (EUROPA) GmbH.
Im Hulsenfeld 13 4010 Hilden, West Germany Tel. 02103-5005-0

SHIMANO (SINGAPORE) PTE. LTD.
No. 20, Benoi Sector, Jurong Town, Singapore 2262 Tel. 2654777
SHIMANO INDUSTRIAL CO.,LTD.
3-77 Oimatsucho, Sakai, Osaka, Japan Tel. (0722) 23-3243

© Jul. 1988. by Shimano. R-97 PIT. SZK. Printed in Japan (English)

Shimano Connecting Pin

SERVICE INSTRUCTIONS

SPECIAL CONNECTING PIN FOR NARROW-TYPE CHAIN

Before use, read these instructions carefully, and follow them for correct use.

Note

- This connecting pin and the reinforced special pin are especially designed for the narrow type of chain.
  They cannot be used for any chain other than the narrow type of chain.

The narrow type of chain is embossed with the word "NARROW"

- For connection, use the type of tool (such as the tool for the Shimano UG chain) that directly presses in the chain.
  Punch type cannot be used.

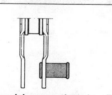

OK   **Do not use**

SHIMANO UG CHAIN TOOL   **PLIER TYPE CHAIN TOOL**

- In order to provide greater connection strength, the connecting pin for the narrow-type chain has a special configuration (the diameter of both ends of the pin is larger than the barrel).

Special connecting pin for narrow-type chain   **Former connecting pin**

- Because of the special shape, the chain will be damaged if it is cut where there is a connecting pin (black). The connecting pin can be identified by its flat head and black color.

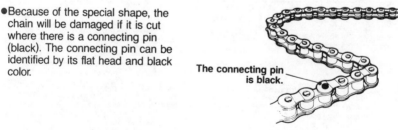

The connecting pin is black.

● To adjust the length of the chain, cut at the end where there is no connecting pin. Do not cut at the end where there is a connecting pin.

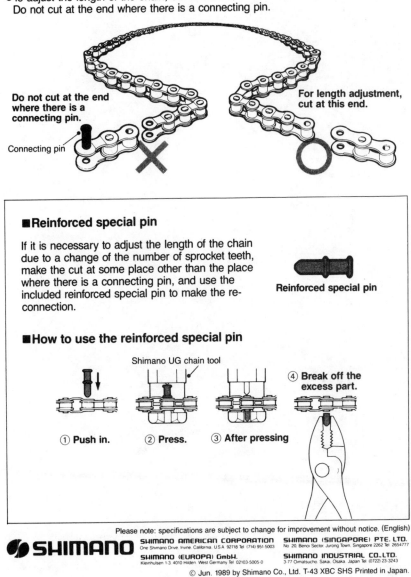

Do not cut at the end where there is a connecting pin.

Connecting pin

For length adjustment, cut at this end.

■**Reinforced special pin**

If it is necessary to adjust the length of the chain due to a change of the number of sprocket teeth, make the cut at some place other than the place where there is a connecting pin, and use the included reinforced special pin to make the re-connection.

Reinforced special pin

■**How to use the reinforced special pin**

Shimano UG chain tool

① **Push in.**   ② **Press.**   ③ **After pressing**   ④ **Break off the excess part.**

Please note: specifications are subject to change for improvement without notice. (English)

SHIMANO

SHIMANO AMERICAN CORPORATION
One Shimano Drive, Irvine, California, U.S.A. 92718 Tel (714) 951-5003

SHIMANO (EUROPA) GmbH.
Klenhulsen 1-3, 4010 Hilden, West Germany Tel 02103-5005-0

SHIMANO (SINGAPORE) PTE. LTD.
No. 20, Benoi Sector, Jurong Town, Singapore 2262 Tel 2654777

SHIMANO INDUSTRIAL CO., LTD.
3-77 Oimatsucho, Sakai, Osaka, Japan Tel (0722) 23-3243

© Jun. 1989 by Shimano Co., Ltd. T-43 XBC SHS Printed in Japan.

INDEX

Note: page numbers in italics refer to illustrations.